SEVEN
STRATEGY
QUESTIONS

ROBERT SIMONS

SEVEN
STRATEGY
QUESTIONS

A SIMPLE APPROACH
FOR BETTER EXECUTION

Harvard Business Review Press

Boston, Massachusetts

Printed in the United States of America

12

No part of this publication may be reproduced, stored in or
introduced into a retrieval system, or transmitted, in any form,
or by any means (electronic, mechanical, photocopying, recording,
or otherwise), without the prior permission of the publisher. Requests
for permission should be directed to permissions@hbsp.harvard.edu,
or mailed to Permissions, Harvard Business School Publishing,
60 Harvard Way, Boston, Massachusetts 02163.

Library of Congress Cataloging-in-Publication Data

Simons, Robert.
    Seven strategy questions : a simple approach for better execution /
Robert Simons.
        p. cm.
    ISBN 978-1-4221-3332-3 (hbk. : alk. paper)   1. Strategic
planning—Management.   2. Business planning—Management.
I. Title.
    HD30.28.S437 2010
    658.4'012—dc22

                                                            2010011510

The paper used in this publication meets the requirements of the
American National Standard for Permanence of Paper for
Publications and Documents in Libraries and Archives Z39.48-1992.

CONTENTS

CONTENTS

INTRODUCTION

Many executives are skeptical of new management techniques. And for good reason. Consultants and the business press are constantly trumpeting new approaches that promise breakthrough performance. But these ideas are often poorly suited to different business situations or not worth the trouble.

I have always worried about the hubris of promoting one-size-fits-all solutions to complex business problems. As a professor at Harvard Business School, I have seen management fads come and go, and I've become leery of prepackaged prescriptions based on the latest theories and techniques.

Writing books and offering high-level consulting advice is easy. Running a business is not. You cannot be aloof and above it all. You must roll up your sleeves and get involved in the details.

There are no easy answers to the issues you face. They are different for every business. But after teaching executives for twenty-five years—facilitating discussions and sharing case studies on successes and failures—I've learned that there is one approach that will add value to every business, including yours: asking the right questions.

TOUGH QUESTIONS FOR BUSINESS LEADERS

The approach of this short book—coaching you to ask yourself and others the right questions to ensure the best implementation of your strategy—is based on three propositions.

First, I believe that executing strategy successfully requires tough, often uncomfortable, choices based on simple logic and clear principles. We often lose sight of these fundamentals in the complexity of techniques and frameworks that consultants and the business press promote in a quixotic attempt to find the magic solution. Simple questions can strip away the confusion that obfuscates clear thinking, allowing us to focus on the key issues that underpin important decisions.

We too often fall into the comfortable habit of avoiding choice in the mistaken belief that we can have it all. Instead of focusing on one primary customer, we have multiple types of customers. Instead of instilling core values, we develop lists of desired behaviors. Instead of focusing on a few critical measures, we build scorecards with an overload of measures. We work hard to avoid making choices.

The questions in this book use counterintuitive arguments to challenge assumptions and force uncomfortable decisions. But they also provide the focus and direction that will assure the successful execution of your strategy.

Second, because every business and industry is unique, it's pointless for me to propose one-size-fits-all solutions to the issues you confront. You know much more about your business than I can ever know.

Finally, to implement strategy successfully, I believe that you must have active discussions with the people in your organization. There is no magic bullet, no metric or scorecard that will tell you where the pitfalls of your business strategy are. There is only one path to success: you must engage in ongoing, face-to-face debate with the people around you about emerging data, unspoken assumptions, difficult choices, and, ultimately, action plans.

The questions in this book should be your constant companion. Carry them as a back-pocket checklist to stimulate strategic thinking. Use them to guide your discussions at strategy retreats and board meetings, where I have seen them used to great success. In day-to-day meetings, you can ask the questions to guide and test subordinates, or to prod superiors to action. Since they demand honest dialogue about business fundamentals and prospects, you should use them as a catalyst for engaging people in the decisions that your company makes.

You—and the people around you—should be able to give consistent, clear answers to these questions. Then, and only then, can you be confident that you're on track for successful implementation of your company's strategy.

SEVEN QUESTIONS

I have purposely kept this book concise. If I could, I would prefer to simply hand you a laminated page with the seven key questions.

I should emphasize two points about these questions. First, they focus on how to execute your business strategy, not how to formulate it. The path you have chosen to create value for your customer and differentiate your products and services is the starting point—a given. But, if your strategy is poorly conceived, the questions will expose those deficiencies and force you to sharpen your thinking.

Second, these questions are not a random list, either in how they are presented or in how they were developed. I present the questions—which you can recall easily if you remember seven C's—in the following sequence: The first two questions (customer, core values) test whether you've built a strong *foundation* for strategy execution.

Seven Strategy Questions

1. Who is your primary customer?

2. How do your core values prioritize shareholders, employees, and customers?

3. What critical performance variables are you tracking?

4. What strategic boundaries have you set?

5. How are you generating creative tension?

6. How committed are your employees to helping each other?

7. What strategic uncertainties keep you awake at night?

The next two (critical performance variables, constraints) address your ability to *focus* everyone's attention on your strategic agenda. Questions five and six (creative tension, commitment) ask whether you have done enough to *facilitate* the behaviors needed for success. The final question (contingencies) focuses on the *future* and your company's ability to adapt to change.

The development of these questions began twenty-five years ago with an intensive study of performance management systems. Over a ten-year period, I interviewed scores of executives, wrote case studies describing successes and failures, and published papers outlining the techniques senior executives use to balance innovation and control. I summarized this work in my book *Levers of Control*.

Next, I turned my attention to the second big topic of strategy implementation: organization design. After more than five years studying prominent executives and how they created structures and accountability systems to deploy resources efficiently in their organizations, I published the results of this work in a second book, *Levers of Organization Design*.

Together, these two books—the first focusing on systems and the second on structure—highlight seven variables that, in my opinion, are the keys to successful strategy implementation in any business.

Turning these variables into the right questions was the final, and most critical, step. Over several years, I worked with executive teams, such as those at Daiichi-Sankyo, Henkel, Honeywell, Lockheed Martin, Marriott, A.P. Moller-Maersk, and Standard Chartered to test and refine the questions. Most recently, these seven questions have formed the backbone of the strategy implementation curriculum in Harvard's Advanced Management Program: this book will allow you to engage the same approach and materials that I use with executive participants in this program.

IMPLEMENTATION IMPERATIVES

Why are these seven questions so vital to your company's success? Each is the crux of a larger "implementation imperative"—a topic or process that you must learn to successfully implement your strategy. I do not use the word *imperative* lightly. Some executives master these imperatives, allowing them to execute winning strategies. Others fail to do so, exposing their business to significant risk.

The importance of these imperatives is driven home when you consider *Lessons from the Top*, a book published ten years ago that profiles fifty top business leaders.[1] Its stories are compelling, and its lessons seem worth learning.

When I read down the list of names—Michael Dell, Bill Gates, Lou Gerstner—I get an uneasy feeling in the pit of my stomach, however. Mixed in with these business luminaries is another set that includes executives such as Bob Eaton (DaimlerChrysler), Hank Greenberg (AIG), and Frank Raines (Fannie Mae).

This second group is not associated with success, but with failure. Each of these executives, we know in hindsight, followed a strategy that ultimately failed. The only lessons here are in figuring out how to avoid similar mistakes!

The seven questions—and the imperative each represents—will help you avoid the pitfalls that trapped these formerly successful executives. Here's a preview of what each chapter of this book will cover, the questions, and their larger imperatives:

Who Is Your Primary Customer?

The first imperative—and the heart of every successful strategy implementation—is *allocating resources to customers*. Continuously competing demands for resources—from business units, support functions, and external partners—require a method for judging whether the allocation choices you have made are optimal.

Therefore, the most critical strategic decision for any business is determining who it is you are trying to serve. Clearly identifying your primary customer will allow you to devote all possible resources to meeting their needs and minimize resources devoted to everything else. This is the path to competitive success.

It's easy to try to duck the tough choice implied by the adjective *primary* by responding that you have more than one type of customer. This answer is a guaranteed recipe for underperformance: the competitor that has clarity about its primary customer and devotes maximum resources to meet their specific needs will beat you every time.

How Do Your Core Values Prioritize Shareholders, Employees, and Customers?

Along with identifying a primary customer, you must also define your core values in a way that ranks the priority of shareholders, employees, and customers. Value statements that are lists of aspirational behaviors aren't good enough. Real core values indicate whose interest comes first when faced with difficult trade-offs.

Prioritizing core values should be the second pillar of your business strategy. For some companies, shareholders come first. For others, it may be employees. In other companies, it may be customers. There is no right or wrong, but choosing is necessary. To illustrate this point, I'll contrast Merck's $20 billion decision to pull Vioxx from the market with Pfizer's decision to continue marketing Celebrex.

What Critical Performance Variables Are You Tracking?

Once you're confident that the foundation of your implementation is sound—you've allocated resources correctly and provided guidance for tough decisions—it's time to get everyone who works for you focused on the job at hand.

Tracking performance goals—the third implementation imperative—requires you to set the right goals, assign accountability, and monitor performance. It's easy to fail this imperative by focusing on the wrong performance indicators or monitoring scorecards that have an overload of irrelevant measures. Underperformance is the result.

It's your job to ensure that your managers are tracking the right things by singling out those variables that spell the difference between strategic success and failure. Like the preceding two questions, the focus in this question is again on an adjective, this time the word *critical*. I will show you a simple but counterintuitive technique that you can use to be sure you're tracking the right things, and I will describe how companies such as Nordstrom and Apple illustrate some unorthodox performance measurement choices that provide the pathway to superior results.

What Strategic Boundaries Have You Set?

Every strategy brings with it the risk that an individual's actions will pull the business off course. Here again, it's easy to fail to inoculate the business against this risk. As we will see, the trick is in setting clear boundaries.

Controlling strategic risk is the fourth implementation imperative. Strategic boundaries—which are always stated in the negative—ensure that the entrepreneurial initiative of your employees aligns with the desired direction of the business. Strategic boundaries can also protect you from the types of errant actions that destroyed Enron and brought financial service firms such as Fannie Mae and Lehman Brothers to their knees.

How Are You Generating Creative Tension?

Once you're satisfied that you are tracking the right performance goals and controlling strategic risk, it's time to turn to the fifth implementation imperative: *spurring innovation*. This imperative is woven into the fabric of every healthy organization, and we all know that companies that fail to innovate will eventually die. No company is immune.

But sustaining ongoing innovation in organizations is notoriously difficult. People fall into comfortable habits, sticking with what they know and rejecting things that cause them to change their ways.

To overcome such inertia, you must push people out of their comfort zones and spur them to innovate. I will provide a menu of techniques you can use to generate creative tension to ensure that everyone is thinking and acting like a winning competitor.

How Committed Are Your Employees to Helping Each Other?

For most companies, it's critically important to build norms so that people will help each other succeed— especially when you're asking people to innovate. But there are exceptions. Some organizations can, and should, be built on self-interest, with every man or woman working for him- or herself.

I suspect that the choice between commitment to help others and self-interest is deeply ingrained in your organization, yet has never been discussed. But if you haven't addressed this choice explicitly—and worked to make it happen—you have increased the potential that your strategy implementation will fail.

Building commitment is the sixth implementation imperative. I will offer a menu of techniques to foster commitment to achieving shared goals. Or, if rewarding self-interest is more appropriate for your business, I will explore alternative approaches you should employ.

What Strategic Uncertainties Keep You Awake at Night?

No matter how good your current strategy is, it won't work forever. There will be booms and busts, customer preferences will change, competitors will introduce new products, and disruptive new technologies will emerge in unexpected places.

This brings us to the final implementation imperative: *adapting to change*. Adapting is critical to survival, but it's extremely difficult to do. With change constantly surrounding us, employees often do not know where to look or how to respond.

I will consider the techniques that companies such as Johnson & Johnson use to search for new information and ideas as markets inevitably change. Your personal attention is the critical catalyst to focus your entire organization on the strategic uncertainties that keep *you* awake at night. After all, everyone watches what the boss watches. I will discuss how you can use this principle to guide the emergence of new strategies for the future.

ENGAGING YOUR ORGANIZATION

In the remainder of this book, you will learn questions you can ask to engage people in fruitful discussion. But these questions are just raw materials. How you interact with the people who report to you—the process you follow—is extremely important.

My work with successful executives has shown that if you want to truly engage people by using these questions, you must follow some commonsense rules:

- You must pose the questions face to face. "Look me in the eye" human interaction is essential for engagement. There is no substitute. You cannot do this remotely or by e-mail. The questioning process derives its power from people rolling up their sleeves and working side by side to solve problems and seize opportunities. You must be able to watch the subtle signals of body language that will tell you when to challenge, probe, and push, and when to offer encouragement and support.

- Discussions must cascade down the organization. They shouldn't be limited to the top, but instead woven into the fabric of your company. If you are consistent in your approach, people at lower levels will mimic your questions in preparation for their upcoming meetings with you. The tone that you set will be replicated throughout the business.

- The process must truly "engage" operating managers. This is the whole point. Staff groups can play a useful role in data input, facilitation, and follow-up, but engagement necessarily involves operating managers who are responsible for results and can commit to action. You should not delegate these questions to staff groups or routine reports. You must demand the full attention of the people who actually run the business.

- Debate must be about what is right, not who is right. People should check titles and office politics at the door. You should encourage everyone to take risks, state unpopular opinions, and challenge the status quo. The success of the process will depend entirely on your commitment to acknowledge and reward innovative thinking. Remember, everyone will be watching you in order to calibrate the risks and rewards of voicing new ideas.

- You must root every discussion in, "What are you going to do about it?" You should think of the questions in this book as the means to an end. They are tools that you can use to stimulate a new, more focused understanding of critical business issues. But the purpose of your engagement is to generate decisions and, ultimately, action.

A WARNING

Peter Drucker once said, "The most serious mistakes are not being made as a result of wrong answers. The truly dangerous thing is asking the wrong questions."

My job is to teach you the right questions to ask and to help you understand why each represents a make-or-break choice for your business. Your job is to engage people throughout your organization in debate and dialogue to find the answers that will allow your business to succeed.

I should warn you that my intention is to be provocative. In the spirit of the Socratic method, a defining feature of our Harvard classroom discussions, I want to challenge your thinking. You may not agree with every position that I take; in fact, you may strenuously disagree with some. But by using these questions, this book will help you identify the unstated assumptions that, if poorly conceived, can sap your business of its energy and potential, and then help you find ways to tighten your thinking so your business thrives.

ONE

WHO IS YOUR PRIMARY
CUSTOMER?

The next time you drive by a McDonald's, take a close look. McDonald's is a company that has reinvented itself. The Golden Arches look the same as they did a decade ago, but the company inside is very different. By carefully identifying its primary customer and allocating resources accordingly, McDonald's has shown continued success even through the downturn that began in 2008.

The growth of McDonald's during its fifty-year history has been described as the greatest retail expansion boom in the history of the world.[1] With good reason. McDonald's 32,000 restaurants feed 58 million customers a day.

What was McDonald's recipe for success? Its worldwide operations reflected a decision that all successful companies make, but rarely discuss or make explicit. The company defined clearly who its primary customer was. Its choice may surprise you. The primary customer was not you and me or our children—the people who eat in its restaurants. Instead, the primary customer at McDonald's was multisite real estate developers and franchise owners. By focusing the bulk of its resources on serving the needs of these developers and multisite franchisees, McDonald's opened as many as seventeen hundred new stores per year. This formula led to year-after-year growth that fueled the company's success over decades.

But in 2003, the company was in crisis. Same-store sales were declining, and growth had ground to a halt. The magic formula was no longer working. Worldwide markets were saturated, and people were tiring of McDonald's standardized fare. This crisis would require a new CEO—Jim Cantalupo—to right the ship. After analyzing the situation, Cantalupo made a fateful decision. From this point forward, he declared, "the new boss at McDonald's is the consumer."[2]

This is one of the most strategic, make-or-break decisions that any company can make. Why? Because defining your primary customer determines how you allocate your resources. The idea is simple: allocate all possible resources to meet and exceed the needs of your primary customer. Conversely, minimize the resources dedicated to everything that does not create value—directly or indirectly—for your customer.

How did McDonald's allocate resources over the many decades that real estate developers were the primary customer? The company created large, centralized corporate functions to support real estate development, franchising, and procurement. But would this same distribution of resources still work now that it had redefined the primary customer as the consumer? The answer, of course, was no. Consumers' tastes differ widely by region, not only within the United States, but also across the many countries where McDonald's operates. To satisfy these varying tastes, McDonald's was forced to reorganize.

Instead of monolithic corporate functions, McDonald's allocated a far greater proportion of its resources to regional managers who were encouraged to customize local menus and store amenities. As a result, McDonald's today offers healthier foods (salads and apple slices) as well as items that cater to regional tastes. In the United Kingdom, McDonald's is serving porridge for breakfast; in Portugal, it offers soup; in France, it's burgers with French cheeses. McDonald's has replaced bolted-down yellow plastic chairs with lime-green designer furniture and dark leather upholstery. The Paris design center offers nine different design options for franchisees to customize the décor for their location and clientele.[3]

Consumer comments suggest the decision to refocus resources is paying off: "Chris Ward says he's a regular again because his McDonald's is open until 1 a.m. Casey Fillian and her friend Carol Milano, now moms, say they often bring their children to the playroom and feel no guilt serving them apple slices and white-meat Chicken McNuggets. Russ Green was drawn back in . . . because McDonald's lattes are cheaper and more convenient than those at Starbucks."[4]

It's no accident that McDonald's was one of only two U.S. companies that ended 2008 with a gain in its stock price (the other was Walmart).[5] As of January 2010, McDonald's has delivered eighty-one consecutive months of increasing global same-store sales.[6] Its current executive team continues to respond to Cantalupo's challenge to make McDonald's "our customers' favorite place and way to eat."[7]

The company's successful turnaround is an example of the importance of the first implementation imperative: *allocating resources to customers*. If you get this wrong, nothing else can make up for your error.

In this chapter, I review the steps that should be the foundation for all your major resource-allocation decisions. The starting point is to ask yourself (and others) the most basic, and important, question for any business strategy: Who is your primary customer?

When confronted with this question, it's easy to answer simply, "We have multiple customers." But this answer is a recipe for underperformance since it ducks the issue highlighted by the adjective *primary*. If you try to serve multiple customers in a single

Who Is Your Primary Customer?

business, you will be forced to spread your resources across too many functions and units in an attempt to meet different customer needs. This "peanut butter" approach to resource allocation—spreading resources evenly over everything—will result in a lack of focus where it really matters.

If your competitors are dedicating every ounce of their resources to create a laser-like focus on a single primary customer, they will beat you every time. Think about it. If you were a potential customer, who would you choose to serve your needs—the business that gives you 100 percent of its attention and resources, or the one that gives you only a fraction?

The old McDonald's prospered for many years by focusing the bulk of its resources on its clearly defined *primary* customer: multisite franchise owners and real estate developers. When this approach stopped working, the company redefined its primary customer and reallocated resources accordingly. Clarity about who its primary customer was—at each stage in its evolution—has provided the foundation for continued growth and profitability.

Attempting to serve multiple types of customers within a single business can mean only one thing: you will serve no customer well. This result was evident at Home Depot after Bob Nardelli, CEO between 2001 and 2007, concluded that the consumer home improvement business was saturated and shifted resources to cater to professional contractors. Home handymen would no longer be the primary customer. Home Depot laid off customer service employees—the ones wearing the orange aprons at its nineteen hundred stores—and replaced the experienced plumbers, electricians, and carpenters employed to answer home owners' questions with part-timers. It reallocated the resources saved through staff cuts to an $8 billion acquisition spree of thirty wholesale housing-supply companies, nearly doubling company revenue.

The effects of the peanut-butter principle were predictable. There were not enough resources to go around—there never are—and neither consumers nor professional contractors were well served. During Nardelli's tenure, consumer satisfaction scores suffered the biggest drop ever recorded for a U.S. retailer. Meanwhile, the new wholesale supply operation was not getting sufficient resources to drive the efficiencies needed in this low-margin business.

It took a new CEO, Frank Blake, to refocus Home Depot by announcing that home owners would again be the primary customer. Home Depot sold the wholesale businesses, increased the number of orange aprons on the floor, and rehired master trade specialists to provide how-to advice to consumers. Customer satisfaction scores and same-store sales and profits have begun to climb (but Blake acknowledged that it will take time to rebuild confidence among customers who switched to competitor Lowe's—a company that never took its eyes off the needs of consumers).[8]

Who should you choose as your primary customer? Your choice will depend on the history of your firm and its founders, the preferences and skills of executives, the nature and intensity of competition, the availability of technical resources, and emerging opportunities that only you can see. My work suggests that the sweet spot for choosing a primary customer is usually found at the intersection of these three variables: perspective, capabilities, and profit potential (see figure 1).

FIGURE 1

Sweet spot for choosing a primary customer

Perspective represents your business's history, folklore, and the personal values of your executives. It provides the lens through which you see business opportunities. Perspective makes it unlikely that McDonald's executives would consider opening high-end French cuisine restaurants. It's also a safe bet that Ferrari won't soon be building budget mass-market cars.

Capabilities refer to the resources—both tangible and intangible—at your disposal. These include physical plant, infrastructure networks, and know-how. Capabilities make it easy for Kraft Foods to market a Kool-Aid line extension to kids, but difficult to challenge Coca-Cola in the soft drink market.

Profit potential is the rate of economic return to be earned from different alternatives. As my colleague Mike Porter has demonstrated, the relative power of buyers, suppliers, competitors, new entrants, and substitute products determines who earns profit in competitive markets.[9] These forces have allowed Intel and Microsoft to extract much of the profit from the personal computing market and are now allowing Google to extract the bulk of the profit in online advertising.

If you are having trouble identifying your primary customer, two issues may be standing in your way: clarifying who is *not* a customer and trying to please other constituents.

CLARIFYING WHO IS NOT
A CUSTOMER

Customers rightfully expect the undivided attention and resources of businesses that compete to serve their needs. So it's vitally important to be clear about who is—and who is not—a customer.

Several years ago at Harvard, we inadvertently created problems for ourselves when we told students in a welcoming assembly that they were customers. This well-meaning compliment backfired when they began acting like customers: complaining about inexperienced junior professors, lobbying for changes in course materials, and demanding that their wishes determine how resources were allocated within the school.

Who is our primary customer? We have made the same choice that all research-based universities make. Our primary customer is the academic experts in various disciplines who use the ideas and new knowledge Harvard generates. Students are important, but their role is different. They are participants in an interactive education process where new research and ideas are presented, tested, and used to enliven classroom discussions.

You may disagree with this decision, or my analysis. But the point is that the reason this decision is so critical for us—and for you—is that it becomes the guiding light for determining how to allocate resources. Since our overriding goal is to create knowledge for academic experts, we organize ourselves and allocate resources by academic specialty: finance professors sit together as a group, strategy professors are organized as a separate unit, leadership professors are separate, and so on. If we had chosen students as our primary customer—an alternative followed by some universities that place less emphasis on research—we would distribute resources differently, perhaps by creating regional campuses close to local communities.

As this example illustrates, identifying your primary customer can be tricky because sometimes the individuals or organizations that use your products, and ultimately pay for them, may not actually be your primary customer. This is more common than you might think. At Mary Kay Cosmetics, for example, the primary customer is not the consumer who uses and pays for Mary Kay products. The company instead allocates the bulk of its resources—through training, product support, and distribution centers—to the needs of the independent beauty consultants who contract with Mary Kay as sales agents. These entrepreneurs purchase Mary Kay products, which they in turn resell to consumers. Mary Kay is successful because it allocates resources with the consultants in mind, rather than catering directly to the end consumer.

You may have also learned the hard way that the word *customer* should be reserved for external constituents, and never used for internal functions or units. Bill George, former CEO of Medtronic, described what can happen if you are not clear-headed about this restriction. Medtronic had adopted a quality program championed by a well-known consulting firm. A critical component of its approach was the creation of internal customers so that, for example, the distribution center was the customer of manufacturing. The unintended consequence was a shift in focus away from external customers to internal customers. As soon as George realized the implications of this mistake, he declared that there would no longer be such a thing as an internal customer.[10]

The danger of ignoring this principle was evident in AOL's ill-fated merger with Time Warner. In seeking to cross-promote its entertainment products, the merged company became its own largest customer for in-house advertising. As a result, it devoted a significant portion of corporate resources to serving the needs of internal units. Because of this inward focus, it badly misallocated resources. As AOL founder Steve Case later admitted, the focus on internal customers caused the company to lose sight of its 30 million external subscribers at a critical juncture in the company's evolution.[11]

Toyota executives were also seduced by the siren song of internal customers. In 2007, CEO Katsuaki Watanabe stated, "'Customer first' is one of the company's core tenets. We don't mean just the end customer; on the assembly line the person at the next workstation is also your customer." After reeling from the largest losses in its history (and, later, severe worldwide quality problems), in part by ignoring what its real customers valued, Watanabe resigned in June 2009 and was replaced by Akio Toyoda. One of the new CEO's first promises was to strengthen the "customer first" philosophy by focusing the business on its real customers.[12]

TRYING TO PLEASE OTHER CONSTITUENTS

The second reason often given for not choosing a primary customer is to avoid offending other constituents—both internal and external—who don't make the cut. Tensions can build among competing interests. Multiple groups want your attention and resources. But you must make choices.

Consider Amazon, the online retailer that now accounts for over 6 percent of the entire U.S. retail market, and a company that maintains a laser-like focus on its primary customer, strategically setting other groups aside. Amazon has two major sources of revenue: direct-to-consumer retail sales and fees from independent retailers that use Amazon to host their storefronts.

These third-party retailers include everything from small mom-and-pop operations to Target, Gap, and Eddie Bauer. They now provide more than one-third of Amazon's revenue.[13] During its formative years, when third-party fees were generating an increasing proportion of revenue, Amazon executives struggled with who they should designate as their primary customer. The company decided firmly in favor of the consumer. It now dedicates all possible resources to reflect this choice.

CEO Jeff Bezos commented on how he resolves the issue when competing interests are at odds, "Whenever we're facing one of those too-hard problems where we can't decide what to do, we try to convert it into a straightforward problem by saying, 'What's better for the consumer?'"[14]

This choice, like other make-or-break decisions I discuss in later chapters, will sometimes require difficult conversations. For Amazon, the flip side of an unrelenting focus on consumers is the occasional unhappiness of third-party retailers who complain that Amazon is not dedicating enough attention to their needs. Some have even filed lawsuits in attempts to force Amazon to devote more resources to their interests.[15] But Amazon has held firm. It continues to allocate resources primarily to its consumer customers. The result: the highest customer-loyalty rating for any retailer in America (and second only to Heinz in customer satisfaction for all U.S. companies of any kind).[16]

UNCOVERING CUSTOMER PREFERENCES

Once you've defined who your primary customer is, you must ensure that you and everyone in your business understand what that customer values. Some customers value low price, others value customized service, while others value world-class technology. Everyone in your company should be aware of, and dedicated to, those preferences.

The downfall of General Motors is a reminder of what can happen if you ignore this requirement. The company basically propelled itself into bankruptcy by building cars that consumers didn't want to buy. Instead of configuring cars to reflect customer demand, GM built vehicles to fill its production plants. As a result, trucks with undersized engines sat unsold in dealer lots, SUVs with winter traction options were shipped to Florida, and midpriced family sedans were overloaded with expensive options. In February 2007, GM had more than 1 million unsold vehicles on dealer lots.

Who does a good job of uncovering customers' values? Procter & Gamble has a reputation for investing heavily in understanding the needs of its primary customers. When A. G. Lafley took over as CEO in 2000, he discovered that the company had lost focus on its customer and was losing market share as a result. One of his first acts was to institute the "consumer is boss" standard that would define his leadership. Soon, over 70 percent of P&G executives participated in a "Living It" program where they spent several days in a consumer's home, eating meals with the family, and accompanying them on shopping trips in order to understand their needs and how they use the consumer products that affect their lives.[17]

Other companies—Walt Disney, Continental Airlines, Sysco, and Amazon, to name only a few—also require executives to regularly spend time performing frontline jobs. The purpose of these initiatives: to force managers and executives to interact with customers and learn firsthand what they value.[18]

Figuring out what your customer values has become more important as businesses are expanding around the globe. Understanding the beauty needs of China's 450 million women is big business by any standard. That's why Estée Lauder has opened a research center in Shanghai, and L'Oréal interviews over thirty-five thousand Chinese women a year (learning, for example, that with water in short supply, it's necessary to reformulate shampoos to rinse out easily).[19]

Choosing a primary customer and understanding what that customer values is important not only for consumer companies, but also for industrial firms, trading firms, and technology firms. Consider two examples: IBM and FedEx. A key part of Lou Gerstner's turnaround strategy was to ask all IBM executives to visit key customers. After these visits, he required executives to analyze their customer's business and make recommendations for configuring IBM's products and services to serve their needs. These white papers became the touchstone within IBM to build a new understanding of which products and services major business customers most valued—and to decide how to allocate resources in the future.[20]

FedEx follows a different approach. The top fifty FedEx executives meet each year for a "Customer Summit," where they invite business customers to give direct face-to-face feedback on what the company is doing well and where it could improve, and also to provide examples of where competitors are doing better. As a senior FedEx executive explained, "We spend a lot of time with those customers listening to their needs, and then we re-allocate resources and dedicate ourselves to improving the areas we find weak."[21]

BUILDING AWARENESS OF CUSTOMER NEEDS

Here's a follow-up question to ask yourself and your colleagues when considering how to allocate resources correctly: does everyone know what your primary customer values? It's not enough that people in your marketing department or a few senior executives share this knowledge. You must constantly remind everyone—from the top of your organization to the bottom—of the importance of truly understanding and responding to your customer's needs.

At P&G headquarters, the focus on the needs of consumers permeates everything P&G does. The lobby is decorated with photographs of consumers using P&G brands. During meetings, P&G encourages managers to ask, "Who is your WHO?" as a shorthand way of describing their primary customer and what makes them tick.[22] Sometimes, managers go as far as creating a cardboard cutout of a fictional customer and putting it at the head of the table as they discuss product attributes.[23] Victoria's Secret—the intimate lingerie division of Limited Brands—does something similar. Executives will often ask each other, "What would Victoria prefer?" knowing full well that Victoria is a fictional persona created to embody brand cachet.

Ford has also recently adopted a similar approach. The company focused its design study for the new Ford Fiesta—its first global platform—on Antonella, an imaginary twenty-eight-year-old woman living in Rome. Her fictional life and preferences provide the backdrop for key design choices.[24]

> Does Everyone Know What Your Primary Customer Values?

ORGANIZING FOR CUSTOMERS

Now for the main point of this chapter. Once you have chosen your primary customer and understood their needs, you must ensure that the bulk of your company's resources is dedicated to one thing and one thing only: providing what your primary customer values. If your business is not deploying resources in a way that maximizes the benefits your customer seeks, someone else will.

Amazon's Bezos reminds people of this threat at every opportunity: "I tell everyone in our business, 'You should wake up every morning terrified with your sheets drenched in sweat, but not because you're afraid of your competitors. Be afraid of your customers because those are the folks who have the money.'"[25] Amazon has used this customer paranoia to justify billions of dollars of investment (critics say overinvestment) in areas that executives believe are important to consumers, including advanced website technology and distribution centers that are industry models of efficiency.[26]

This prompts another—and vitally important—follow-up question: How have you organized to deliver maximum value to your customer?

Your answer will depend, of course, on the needs of your primary customer. Different customers require different organization designs.

To illustrate this central point, consider two seemingly similar companies: Visa and MasterCard. Even though they compete in the same industry, each has chosen a different primary customer. As a result, the two businesses have organized in very different ways. MasterCard has defined its primary customer as large global banks like JPMorgan Chase and Citigroup. These customers value low price. To serve its customers' needs, MasterCard has centralized its resources to maximize global efficiency and drive down transaction costs. Visa, by contrast, has chosen regional banks with local preferences as its primary customer. Visa competes by customizing programs and card offerings to meet its customers' different needs. As a result, Visa has organized its resources by region. Not surprisingly, when these two companies went public, they did so in different ways. MasterCard created a single, global holding company. Visa carved out its European operation as a separate entity controlled by its member banks.[27]

> How Have You Organized to Deliver Maximum Value to Your Customer?

Different firms make different choices about how to organize resources to best serve their specific customer needs. Walmart's customers value low price, so the company has organized by function to drive economies of scale. Nestlé's customers around the world have varying preferences for sweets and spices, so it organizes by country to respond to local tastes. IBM focuses on integrated services, so it has created dedicated relationship teams at the center of its organization design.

What about large, diversified groups that have more than one type of customer? Such companies—GE comes to mind as an example—create separate product divisions dedicated to the needs of each customer group. Then, each division or business unit can organize its resources in whatever way best meets the needs of its different primary customers.

Pepsi followed this principle when it split itself in two in 1999. When facing competing demands for attention from consumers and retailers, it spun off its bottler operations as a separate company. PepsiCo, the concentrate manufacturer, could then focus attention on product development and marketing to its primary customer: consumers. The newly separate bottling group could focus its resources on retailers that value something quite different: price, consistency, and responsiveness.

In 2009, Pepsi reversed this decision by reacquiring its major bottlers.[28] Pepsi CEO Indra Noori claimed that reintegrating the businesses would allow more responsiveness to the changing tastes of consumers who were abandoning carbonated drinks in favor of juices and waters.[29] But like any choice, this decision will have consequences. It's a safe bet that the newly integrated company will reduce the resources it devotes to retailers, which will again be treated as constituents rather than primary customers.

None of these examples is meant to imply that you should never change your primary customer. At times, this kind of bold change is essential. But you need to recognize the critical importance of this decision. Changing your primary customer invariably means that you should also be making a fundamental shift in your resource allocation and organization design.

Recall the McDonald's story that opened this chapter. Cantalupo's decision to change the primary customer from real estate developers to consumers was the foundation for a turnaround that propelled the company out of crisis. By reallocating resources from the operating core to regional managers, executives were able to support consumer-focused innovation that transformed the company.

Of course, you don't have to (and shouldn't) wait for a crisis before altering course. Cisco is an example of a company that has successfully navigated the transformation from one primary customer to another as part of an ongoing evolution. Following a string of rapid acquisitions during the dot.com era, the company ended up with too many separate businesses and too many different types of customers. Attention and resources were dispersed and diluted.

So Cisco reinvented itself by redefining its primary customer as channel partners—businesses that resell its technology products. This strategic change required a fundamental restructuring of the business. No longer a collection of independent business units, Cisco now claims it's the world's biggest functionally aligned organization. Centralization of the operating core has streamlined operations, cut costs, and delivered what its primary customers value—cutting-edge technology deployed at lowest possible prices. The new orientation has been a success. Channel partners now account for 92 percent of Cisco's sales.[30]

CONTROLLING STAFF RESOURCES

So far, I have focused on meeting the needs of your primary customer. But what about your other constituents? How should you meet their needs?

The answer is simple, but again requires the resolve to make a hard choice. You should delegate responsibility for serving your other constituents to staff groups: investor relations, human resources, and regulatory affairs. These units can then use their specialized expertise to meet the needs of your constituents. This allocation of resources has the advantage of freeing up the rest of your organization to focus on creating value for your primary customer.

The hard part is deciding on the right level of funding for staff units. On the one hand, you want to allocate sufficient resources to allow staff specialists to meet the legitimate needs of your various constituents. But, on the other hand, there's a substantial risk that staff groups will receive too many resources—resources that you could better utilize serving customers. You don't want—or need—gold-plated staff groups.

If your goal is to maximize the resources you devote to your primary customer, the corollary is clear. You should minimize resources you devote to everything else. Serve their legitimate needs, but no more. Have you minimized resources devoted to your other constituents?

You should continually be testing whether you have this balance right. Is there room to reduce the resources that do not serve customers directly—by streamlining and managing smarter—and rededicate those resources to customers?

Have You Minimized Resources Devoted to Your Other Constituents?

Look at your overhead expenses as a percent of revenue. How do they compare to best practices in your industry? Are they too high? If so, you should make it a priority to redistribute excess staff resources to activities that create value for your customer.

Jamie Dimon followed this principle when he took over as CEO of JPMorgan Chase. One of his first decisions was to consolidate the bank's computer systems and bring outsourced information technology systems inside the company. He eliminated more than two thousand support jobs and cut costs dramatically. The capital freed up from this consolidation was then used to fund new customer-focused growth initiatives that included the hiring of three thousand new salespeople.[31] Using a similar approach, Kasper Rorsted, CEO of Germany's consumer products company Henkel AG, instituted a "just good enough" standard for the funding of staff groups. His purpose: to ensure that Henkel focuses the bulk of corporate resources on serving its primary customers.

ALLOCATING RESOURCES TO CUSTOMERS

In this chapter, the tough choice is about allocating resources. Choosing your *primary* customer—as difficult as it may be—is the foundation for that allocation, and for every winning strategy.

If there is uncertainty about your primary customer, it can mean only one thing: you are diverting and wasting resources that you should dedicate to your customer. By bringing clarity to your choice of primary customer, understanding what that customer values, and then organizing your company around those needs, you strengthen your company's ability to compete for—and win—that customer.

TWO

· · · · · · ·

HOW DO YOUR CORE VALUES PRIORITIZE SHAREHOLDERS, EMPLOYEES, AND CUSTOMERS?

It was late on Friday afternoon when Ray Gilmartin, CEO of pharmaceutical giant Merck, received the phone call from Dr. Peter Kim, head of Merck's research and development labs.

Kim was calling to inform Gilmartin that the independent safety monitoring board overseeing the thirty-six-month test of Vioxx, Merck's blockbuster arthritis pain medication, was recommending a halt to the research study. For the first eighteen months, there had been no difference in heart attacks and strokes between patients taking Vioxx and those assigned a placebo. But from months eighteen through thirty, there was an unexpected increase in adverse cardiovascular events for patients taking Vioxx.

This was the most carefully controlled study to look at the long-term safety of Vioxx. Several previous studies had suggested that there might be cardiovascular risks, but Merck scientists had conducted careful analyses to confirm that Vioxx was safe.

Gilmartin was surprised to hear the news. Like everyone else at Merck, he believed in the safety and efficacy of Vioxx. His wife took the medication daily, as did Ed Scolnick, prior head of Merck research labs, who had been in charge of the drug's development.

After analyzing data all weekend, Kim came back to Gilmartin on Monday morning with three options. First, Merck could continue the study to its planned conclusion. Six months of additional data would give researchers better information to assess how to proceed. Alternatively, the company could ask the U.S. Food and Drug Administration to approve a black-box warning label for the drug so that prescribing doctors and patients would be fully informed about the drug's newly discovered risks. Such a label change would allow pain sufferers to continue using the drug. The final option was to withdraw Vioxx from the market.

Pulling Vioxx would be a difficult decision. The new Cox-2 inhibitor drugs (Merck's Vioxx and Pfizer's Celebrex) were the only pain medications that provided relief for millions of patients afflicted with chronic arthritis. In addition, the drug generated more than $2.5 billion in annual revenue for Merck. Withdrawing Vioxx from the market would cost the company more than $20 billion in lost profits over its expected life.

On Thursday, September 30, 2004, six days after the initial phone call from Kim, Gilmartin called a press conference to announce the worldwide withdrawal of Vioxx.[1]

Other companies in similar circumstances might have acted differently. But the second implementation imperative—*prioritizing core values*—provided clear guidance to Merck executives about how to make this difficult choice.

Most companies have statements of core values. These shared beliefs and norms can be found on wall placards, company websites, and wallet cards. They typically include traits such as integrity, teamwork, diversity, continuous improvement, and personal accountability.

Such well-meaning lists are a recipe for underperformance. Why? Because they ignore the adjective *core* and obscure the fundamental value that should be the foundation of every successful business. Core values should tell people whose interests to put first when faced with difficult choices.

Defining core values is not just a "feel good" thing to do. It's a critical business decision. This chapter will test whether you've defined your core values properly. If you have, you should have no trouble answering the following question: How do your core values prioritize shareholders, employees, and customers?

How Do Your Core Values Prioritize Shareholders, Employees, and Customers?

When faced with a tough decision—like Merck's decision with Vioxx—do people in your business know which way to turn? Should shareholder profit trump the needs of your customers? Or, do you want managers to decide in favor of employee job security? Or, perhaps your company is dedicated to putting customers first even if it means lower profits for shareholders? The more decentralized you are—allowing people throughout your business to make choices about how to create value and for whom—the more your employees need to know how to make these choices.

The need to prioritize core values is independent of your choice of primary customer. As I discussed in the previous chapter, understanding the needs of your customer determines how you should structure your business and allocate resources. Core values provide guidance, within that structure, on how to make choices when the outcome benefits one set of constituents at the expense of others.

Confusion about core values was at the root of the debacle at Fannie Mae, a publicly traded mortgage financing company with a government-backed mission. Whose interests were supposed to come first: shareholders or customers? Fannie Mae executives—at the behest of politicians—dedicated corporate resources to democratizing home ownership by offering mortgages to those who couldn't otherwise afford them. (You could argue about who the primary customer was in this instance: politicians or home owners.)

As one observer noted approvingly at the time, "Guided and inspired by this purpose, Fannie Mae launched in the early 1990s a series of bold initiatives, including a program to develop new systems for reducing mortgage underwriting costs by 40 percent in five years; programs to eliminate discrimination in the lending process (backed by $5 billion in underwriting experiments); and an audacious goal to provide, by the year 2000, $1 trillion targeted at 10 million families that had traditionally been shut out of home ownership—minorities, immigrants, and low-income groups."[2] We now know, of course, that to achieve these goals, Fannie Mae lowered underwriting and documentation standards to dangerous levels.

At the same time they were allocating resources to home owners, Fannie Mae executives were also attempting to maximize shareholder value (and their own paychecks). To boost reported profits, they built up increasingly risky loan portfolios that were resold with recourse to secondary markets, earning CEO Frank Raines more than $90 million in personal compensation and bonuses.[3] When the housing market collapsed, the cost of these confused choices left American taxpayers with a bailout bill of $100 billion.

THREE CHOICES

When faced with tough choices, some companies put customers first, others put employees on top, and others choose shareholders. Each choice is based on a different theory of value creation. There is no right or wrong. But choosing—and communicating your choice—is essential.

Gilmartin stated that withdrawing Vioxx was "the responsible thing to do." He said, "It's built into the principles of the company to think in this fashion. That's why the management team came to such an easy conclusion."

The principles that Gilmartin referred to were articulated in a 1950 statement by former CEO George W. Merck: "We try never to forget that medicine is for the people. It is not for the profits. The profits follow, and if we have remembered that, they have never failed to appear. The better we have remembered it, the larger they have been."[4]

The decision of executives to withdraw Vioxx was supported by Merck's long-standing mission, "Where patients come first," and a theory that putting customers first would reward owners in the long term.

Not every company chooses to put customers first. Southwest Airlines—like many service-based companies—puts employees first. Former CEO Herb Kelleher stated, "It's sometimes been held out to be a conundrum in business—'Who comes first, employees, customers, or shareholders?' We've never thought it was a conundrum. If employees are treated well, they'll treat the customers well. If the customers are treated well, they'll come back, and the shareholders will be happy."[5] To drive this point home, Kelleher appeared in national newspaper ads under the caption, "Employees first. Customers second. Shareholders third."

This employee-first approach requires hiring the right kind of people. Southwest often interviews over thirty people to find someone with the right attitude to fill even a relatively junior position.[6] Southwest's theory of putting employees first seems to work. It has allowed the company to dominate its industry in both financial performance and shareholders' returns for the past fifteen years.

HCL Industries, an Indian outsourcing company that employs fifty-five thousand employees in seventeen countries, emulated Southwest's approach with its own "Employee First, Customer Second" philosophy. CEO Vineet Nayar believed that an empowered, well-trained workforce was essential in an industry where global customers were looking for value-added solutions. Nayar explained, "Employee First was . . . about setting clear priorities, investing in employees' development, and unleashing their potential to produce bottom-line results. As a services business, the employee interface with the customer was critical."[7]

But HCL was constrained by the rote teaching methods of the Indian education system. So it created an ambitious program of employee engagement. To execute its employee-first approach, executives adopted a 360-degree feedback system that made managers accountable to their direct subordinates, instituted opinion poll voting for decisions that affect employees, and made themselves accountable to follow-up of all employee suggestions.[8]

Some companies don't put customers or employees first. Instead, executives at some companies put shareholders first. Stock price appreciation is the overarching goal for everyone in the business. In an official pronouncement, the Business Roundtable, an organization of CEOs of the largest U.S. companies, explained the rationale for this approach when it argued that the paramount duty of management is to stockholders: "Corporations are often said to have obligations . . . to other constituencies, including employees, the communities in which they do business, and government, but these obligations are best viewed as part of the paramount duty to optimize long-term stockholder value."[9]

Examples of companies that have successfully put shareholders first over long periods of time are hard to find. Critics point to the inevitable short-term orientation caused by the focus on day-to-day stock price changes and the dangers of an ends-justify-the-means philosophy. Jack Welch, one of the first proponents of shareholder value, now speaks vociferously against it, "On the face of it, shareholder value is the dumbest idea in the world. Shareholder value is a result, not a strategy . . . Your main constituencies are your employees, your customers and your products."[10]

Notwithstanding these criticisms, there are situations where putting shareholder interests first may be the right thing to do. Consider trading firms operating in liquid and efficient markets, or private equity firms investing in distressed companies. If you are using shareholder funds for proprietary trades in such markets, it's entirely appropriate to make shareholder profit the overriding core value.

If you do decide to put shareholders first, motivation can be a problem. It's possible to inspire people to serve customers well or to invest in building employee capabilities. But motivating people to work hard to make others rich is another story. Because of this difficulty, companies that put shareholders first invariably use stock ownership, stock options, and bonuses based on EPS growth to motivate effort. The intent is to tie personal wealth to stock price appreciation and thereby motivate managers to make tough decisions that will increase shareholder value by cutting costs, acquiring competitors, and manipulating balance sheet assets and liabilities.

Hank McKinnell, Pfizer CEO and chairman of the Business Roundtable when it issued its statement on the primacy of shareholder value, spent tens of billions of dollars of shareholders' money acquiring competitors, including Warner-Lambert and Pharmacia, in a quest to boost Pfizer stock price. Similarly, Sandy Weill, who tied the compensation of executives who worked for him directly to increases in stock price, was a serial acquirer concerned primarily with increasing the wealth of his shareholders.[11] His success in merging Citicorp and Travelers to form Citigroup was the pinnacle of a career devoted to boosting shareholder value by joining together companies where executives could find synergies to cut costs.

AIG is another example of a company that used stock grants aggressively to motivate people to focus first and foremost on shareholder value. Stock-based incentives prompted employees to create highly leveraged (and highly profitable—at least in the short term) financial products such as credit default swaps. Following the crisis that led to the 2005 ouster of CEO Hank Greenberg, AIG's compensation committee doubled down on its incentive program when it announced "that an additional equity grant should be made to employees, including executive officers, to assist in retention and to provide a direct incentive for employees to focus on shareholder value during this time."[12]

Who should your core values recognize as most important: shareholders, employees, or customers? Each choice is based on a different theory of value creation. Only you can decide what's best for your business. Companies that put customers first believe that a satisfied customer relationship is the key to long-term corporate success. Companies that put employees first—often service-based industries—believe that committed employees will work harder to please customers, building loyalty and superior financial returns. Those that put shareholders first believe that employees should focus on creating value directly by actions that boost operating income, asset utilization, and the asset base of the company.

Which is best? If I wanted to invest for short-term gain, I would probably pick an underperforming company where a new CEO was championing shareholder value. But if I wanted to invest for the long term, my bet would be with the firm whose executives put either customers or employees first. Why? Because of the different decisions that executives can be expected to make under each of these scenarios.

CORE VALUES SHOULD GUIDE DECISIONS

If you define core values properly—with clarity about who comes first—you should have no trouble telling stories that describe tough choices made in keeping with those values. If you can't find such examples, then your values aren't working.

IBM CEO Sam Palmisano cites stories of people in different parts of the world contacting each other for help in solving client problems, and of managers giving up local profit in favor of integrated client solutions. He uses these stories to reinforce IBM's core value of putting client success first. As Palmisano explains, "Values inject balance between the interests of shareholders, employees, and clients. In every case, you have to make a call. Values help you make those decisions, not on an ad hoc basis, but in a way that is consistent with your culture and brand, with who you are as a company."[13]

What Tough Decisions Have Been Guided by Your Core Values?

What tough decisions have been guided by your core values? If your business has clarified who comes first, managers will have no trouble finding such stories. One story, retold many times at Johnson & Johnson, recounts that company's multimillion-dollar decision in the mid-1980s to recall Tylenol from every shelf across the county when tainted bottles were discovered in a single outlet in Chicago. This decision has become part of the folklore at J&J and reminds current employees that they are expected to make tough choices in favor of customers.

Merck's decision to withdraw Vioxx was also a tough choice made in favor of customers. Not only was more than $20 billion of profit at stake, Merck scientists and executives knew that Vioxx was an important drug for pain management. Nevertheless, Merck executives never wavered, even as the company's market value fell $25 billion within hours of the announcement. Clarity in its core value—patients come first—provided clarity for the right thing to do. Although financially painful in the short term, this decision has paid long-term dividends. The public's confidence in Merck is high, and investor returns have rebounded to their original levels.

You may be thinking that the decisions at Johnson & Johnson and Merck were obvious. Human health and lives were at stake. But consider the fact that Pfizer's executives made a different choice. Knowing Celebrex—the Cox-2 inhibitor they acquired when they purchased Pharmacia—also exhibited cardiovascular problems, Pfizer executives decided to keep their drug on the market with a black-box warning and to market its benefits aggressively. Pfizer's shareholders benefited in two ways: by avoiding billions of dollars of lost profit and picking up Merck patients who were forced to give up Vioxx.

Some companies put employees first. If you choose this path, the rubber meets the road in lean economic times. This is when you will be tested to see if you are willing to live with lower profit levels to protect jobs.

Southwest Airlines supports its employees-first philosophy with a no-layoff policy for its thirty-two thousand employees. As CEO Gary Kelly said during the depths of the downturn in 2009, "We've never had a layoff. We've never had a pay cut. And we're going to strive mightily, especially this year, to avoid them once again."[14] The same policy applies at steelmaker Nucor, "We have a no-layoff practice that we have been able to follow going back to 1966," said a Nucor spokesman. "Our no-layoff practice continues even today in the current challenging economic environment. If you go into one of our plants and see our people in action it'll be clear how productive and committed they are."[15]

For companies that put shareholders first, tough decisions typically relate to cost cutting and downsizing to improve financial returns. Executives at John Deere farm equipment, for example, worried that the company was carrying too much inventory and receivables and was not charging customers prices that reflected the value provided. The result was disappointing performance.

To remedy this situation, Deere executives introduced "shareholder-value-added" as the key measure by which to evaluate management performance. They tied bonuses to this measure by formula. The results should be no surprise. Managers sold off the underperforming Homelite chainsaw business and closed a new, gleaming—but underutilized—factory. Another division cut 20 percent of its workforce. Inventories were slashed and receivable collections tightened up. Financial performance improved dramatically.[16]

Who comes first in your business? What stories can you tell to illustrate your core values in action?

RESPONSIBILITY TO OTHER CONSTITUENTS

There is nothing wrong with putting shareholders first, just as there is nothing wrong with putting customers or employees first. Each choice is based on a different theory of value creation. But you can get in trouble by forgetting that your business also has a responsibility to other constituents who are affected by your decisions.

Al Dunlap's quest for creating shareholder value by hyperaggressive cost cutting earned him the nickname "Chainsaw Al." His most notable success was Scott Paper where, in twelve months as CEO, Dunlap fired 35 percent of employees—over ten thousand people—and

70 percent of corporate staff. His actions boosted the stock price from \$38 to \$120 per share, allowing Dunlap to sell the business to Kimberly-Clark for a gain of \$6 billion (with a \$100 million personal payoff). Dunlap's pride in this achievement was evident in the title of his book, *Mean Business*.[17]

Dunlap seemed gleeful as he fired employees and closed factories in the name of boosting shareholder value. But customers also suffered when he chose not to invest in brands or technology. Dunlap was later unceremoniously kicked out of Sunbeam as he drove the business into the ground.

To counter such abuses—that affect the lives of employees and communities—some observers argue that executives have a duty to improve the welfare of all constituents affected by their decisions. Inserting the word *social* into the phrase *corporate responsibility*, proponents of this view believe that executives should allocate some portion of corporate resources to improve the welfare of society at large. Others disagree, claiming that diverting company resources to improve general welfare is not the responsibility of business.

Regardless of where you stand in this debate, you must be clear-headed about the fact that your choice of who comes first—shareholders, employees, or customers—does not give people in your business license to harm others affected by your decisions. Pfizer's decision to continue marketing Celebrex benefited shareholders. But the company also included a black-box warning on the drug so that patients and their doctors could be fully informed about the risks and benefits of the medication. They could then make a fully informed decision.

Do your core values recognize your business's responsibility to others? To ensure that there is no confusion on this point, your values should stipulate the *minimum* level of corporate responsibility that you want people in your business to shoulder.

One approach is to hold everyone in your business accountable to the physician's Hippocratic Oath: Do no harm. In other words, people have a duty to ensure that their actions leave none of your constituents worse off.

> Do Your Core Values Recognize Your Business's Responsibility to Others?

Do no harm may seem like a low standard to meet. It's not. Factories create waste and emissions, new facilities displace old, and employees must be let go in a downsizing. Standards of responsibility differ around the world. But a clear, do-no-harm standard can be your aspiration. Everyone in your company should strive to make it a reality.

Both Walmart and Nike have failed this test in the past. Both have rethought their basic responsibility to others. Nike, which has been accused of labor abuses in developing countries, created a position of vice president of corporate responsibility, reporting directly to the CEO, with a team of over 130 people worldwide. The mission is to drive corporate responsibility goals—enforcing minimum labor standards and promoting sound environmental policies—through all aspects of Nike's operations.[18] In a similar move, Walmart committed to reduce harm by increasing the efficiency of its vehicle fleet by 25 percent in three years and doubling it in ten years, cutting energy use by 30 percent in its stores, reducing solid waste by 25 percent, and investing $500 million in sustainability initiatives.[19]

Of course, there may be strategic reasons to move your business well beyond a do-no-harm standard. Consider Exelon, the largest electric and gas utility in the United States. Even though Exelon's fleet of a dozen nuclear reactors allows it to generate power with relatively low emissions, CEO John Rowe has launched an ambitious strategy to displace more than 15 million tons of greenhouse gas per year by 2020—the equivalent of taking 3 million cars off the roads.[20] As an operator of environmentally sensitive generating facilities, Exelon's rate structure depends critically on the goodwill of the public and politically appointed regulators. For

Exelon—and many other companies in a variety of industries—a strategy of environmental activism is smart business.

Where does your business stand on responsibility to others? Are people clear about their minimum level of responsibility to others?

One of the best examples of getting core values right is exemplified in Johnson & Johnson's credo, which has been in continuous use since 1943. In four detailed paragraphs, J&J's credo explicitly names all the groups for which employees must take responsibility and the appropriate level of care.

The first paragraph begins, "We believe our *first* responsibility is to the doctors, nurses and patients, to mothers and fathers and all others who use our products and services." This definition—which explicitly puts customers first—encompasses the different customers of J&J's businesses.

The next two paragraphs spell out the company's minimum level of responsibilities to employees and communities. The final paragraph states, "Our final responsibility is to our stockholders. Business must make a sound profit. We must experiment with new ideas. Research must be carried on, innovation programs developed and mistakes paid for . . . When we operate according to these principles, the stockholders should realize a fair return."

Johnson & Johnson's credo responds to the three issues I have raised in this chapter by (1) prioritizing customers first, employees and communities second, and shareholders last; (2) providing guidance for tough decisions, such as the Tylenol crisis; and (3) explicitly recognizing the level of responsibility to others that the company wants employees to embrace.

Something else is evident from J&J's credo: a focus on the long term. Management's responsibility to others includes doing no harm not only to people today, but also to those who will follow in future generations. The credo states, for example, "We must maintain in good order the property we are privileged to use, protecting the environment and natural resources." For stockholders, it states, "Reserves must be created to provide for adverse times."

At Johnson & Johnson, the foundation of the credo is responsibility to others. Former CEO Ralph Larsen commented, "If you don't think that the credo is important, or you don't believe in its values, you are not going to last at Johnson & Johnson. The organization will reject you, because sooner or later you will do something that will bring harm to the company. The organization will expel you, just like the body expels foreign organisms. For us, the credo is the North Star. We'll often sit around and try to come up with a course of action and somebody will say, 'How do you square that with the credo?'"[21]

COMMITMENT TO YOUR
CORE VALUES

It's one thing to write the words on paper or print them on a wall plaque. It's quite another to ensure that everyone in your business—from top to bottom—is committed to act in ways that are consistent with those principles.

At senior levels, commitment to core values is tested in two ways. First, by the tough decisions executives make over time: whether or not to withdraw a blockbuster drug with potential health risks, whether or not to maintain full employment in a severe recession, whether or not to sell underperforming divisions to increase shareholder returns.

The second way that values are brought to life is through decisions on promotions and rewards. You can say all the right words and publish inspirational value statements, but if you promote and reward people who behave badly, cynicism will abound. Every promotion you make sends an unambiguous signal about your true values and your commitment to them.

At lower levels, where day-to-day decisions are made, it's more difficult to know if people are committed to your core values. You may have handed out laminated wallet cards, but how do you know if they're really making a difference? Is everyone committed to your core values?

Is Everyone Committed to Your Core Values?
One way to find out is to have staff specialists survey employees about which values they understand and apply. This is good practice and generally worth doing.

But sometimes the answer is right in front of you. Walk around any Johnson & Johnson facility and you won't go far before you find the credo posted on a wall. Managers talk about the credo openly and use it as a benchmark for tough decisions. I understood the importance of this visibility recently when I was teaching an executive class. We were discussing J&J's credo. One of the participants, a senior manager from a prominent defense contractor, put up his hand and told this story:

I'd heard about Johnson & Johnson's credo, but I'd never seen it. I was curious. So, I picked up a box of Band-Aids and looked on the back for the 1-800 number for customer comments and suggestions. I called the number and asked the lady who answered, "Who should I contact to get a copy of your credo?"

"Do you have a fax machine?" she asked me.

"Yes," I replied, and gave her the number. Less than a minute later, a copy of Johnson & Johnson's credo was printing out of my fax.

How would your employees respond to a similar request?

PRIORITIZING CORE VALUES

This chapter introduces the second building block of strategy implementation. As in the previous chapter, I use an adjective, *core*, to remind you that tough choices are necessary.

The core value in any business is choosing whose interests come first when faced with tough decisions and trade-offs. If your core values are providing guidance, you won't have any difficulty telling stories of situations where they have determined people's decisions. If you can't easily find such stories, then your values are not doing their job.

With these two chapters behind us, the foundation of strategy execution is now in place. You have clarified who your primary customer is and allocated resources accordingly. Your core values state whose interests come first, and your employees are clear about how to make tough trade-offs.

The stage is now set. In the next two chapters, we consider how to get everyone focused on your strategic agenda.

THREE

* * * * * * *

WHAT CRITICAL
PERFORMANCE VARIABLES
ARE YOU TRACKING?

Lisa Johnson faced a tough decision. As area manager of Citibank's thirty Los Angeles branches, she had to recommend a year-end evaluation and bonus for James McGaran. McGaran managed the most important branch in the area. Located in the financial district, competition with Bank of America and Wells Fargo branches was intense.

McGaren's financial results were outstanding—20 percent above target. He had generated the highest revenue and greatest margin contribution of any branch in the system.

But there was a problem. Citibank was attempting to differentiate itself in the local market by providing relationship banking with high levels of customer service. To focus everyone on this strategy, Citibank had instituted a new balanced scorecard. In addition to traditional financial measures, the bank had added new measures for five performance variables: strategy implementation, customer satisfaction, control, people, and standards. The most important of these was customer satisfaction. Frits Reiger, group president, considered the customer satisfaction measure a leading indicator of the long-term success of his division.

McGaran's scores on the balanced scorecard's measures were outstanding—with one exception. His customer satisfaction scores were below par. But there were confounding factors to consider: McGaran had the largest and most difficult branch in the division; he faced a demanding clientele and fierce competition; he did not control centralized Citibank services such as ATMs and online banking. Given these constraints, McGaran believed he had done everything possible to improve customer satisfaction. His financial results, he claimed, told the real story.

To compound the problem for Johnson, McGaran's bonus was linked by formula to the new scorecard's results. To be eligible for an overall above-par rating and the highest bonus level, McGaran had to achieve at least par on every measure of the scorecard. Giving him a below-par customer satisfaction score would cut his bonus significantly. Not only was McGaran's pride at stake (he had received a full bonus in previous years), but he was being actively pursued by competitors. Nevertheless, the bank saw its new scorecard—and especially its customer satisfaction measure—as critical to its strategy. Other branch managers were watching the case carefully. Making an exception for McGaran could destroy the integrity of the new measurement system. But there was also a risk that McGaran might quit if the new scorecard system incorrectly calibrated his contribution.[1]

This dilemma reminds us of the power and pitfalls of setting goals, assigning accountability, and monitoring performance. By one measure—revenue—McGaran had performed exceptionally. And many would argue that revenue growth is the ultimate measure of customer satisfaction.

But we're all aware of the limits of using accounting measures such as revenue as arbiters of success. In chapter 1, I alluded to the 1 million unsold vehicles sitting on General Motors dealers' lots. Ignoring customer preferences was at the root of this problem, but GM's revenue-recognition policies allowed it to persist. Instead of waiting until a vehicle was sold to a consumer, GM booked revenue when the vehicle was driven out the factory door. As a result, there were no financial consequences for continuing to build vehicles that consumers didn't want to buy.

Like Citibank, many companies are adopting a broad range of indicators to measure success. Not everyone is happy with this solution. Managers complain that they're overwhelmed and confused by the number of variables and measures they're asked to manage. *Tracking performance goals*—the third implementation imperative—can propel your organization to strategic success. But do it badly and you can derail the entire enterprise.

In this chapter, I review the questions you must ask to ensure that your performance measures are helping, not hindering, the execution of your strategy. The goal is to ensure that your measures and scorecards are focusing everyone on your strategic agenda.

The question—What critical performance variables are you tracking? (with its focus on the adjective *critical*)—is the starting point.

What Critical Performance Variables Are You Tracking?

When I teach the Citibank case to executives, a highly charged debate ensues. Half of the class members argue that Johnson should ignore the rules of the scorecard, ignore the low customer-satisfaction scores, and give McGaran an overall excellent rating with a full bonus. They claim that the scorecard is too new to be reliable, includes too many uncontrollable factors, and is based on too small a sample size. He's a top performer and should be recognized as such.

The other class members dig in their heels. They want to stick with the system to signal the importance of customer satisfaction. McGaran, in their opinion, should get only a par rating overall and his bonus should be cut accordingly. To them, the integrity of the system is more important than one individual's feelings.

The discussion intensifies as individuals argue back and forth about the risk of losing McGaran if he is not properly recognized. At the limit, some feel that Citibank should be willing to let him walk away to signal the importance of the new scorecard measures.

With no solution in sight, I intervene by asking participants how confident they are that the indicators on the Citibank scorecard measure the right variables. In other words, are the five measures on the scorecard—strategy implementation, customer satisfaction, control, people, and standards—the true drivers of revenue growth and profitability? Participants take a break from arguing with each other when they realize that they don't know the answer to my question.

To evaluate the usefulness of any performance measures, you must first decide if they are measuring the right things. Otherwise you may be making important decisions based on the wrong indicators.

There is only one way to test this: you must explain how you believe value is created. Then, and only then, can you determine what variables and measures are critical to success.

FROM A LIST TO A THEORY

If you are currently tracking a bunch of performance indicators that are not explicitly linked to your strategy—as they seem to be doing at Citibank—you will present people with a random list of measures that may or may not make sense to them. How can they (or you) have confidence that you are measuring the right things? The only way to break through this uncertainty is to explain your theory of value creation so that everyone can understand how the different variables fit together.

Figure 2 shows an example of what such a theory of value creation might look like for a consumer retail bank following a high-service strategy.

Reading from left to right, this diagram shows the links among a variety of inputs, processes, and output variables. It illustrates the variables that create a satisfied customer relationship and, ultimately, lead to market share growth and financial performance.

Transforming a list of performance measures into a theory of value creation allows everyone to understand your reasons for selecting the performance variables you track. People can ask questions, test assumptions, and understand why you have chosen some variables and not others.

This hypothetical diagram also provides a lens for assessing the importance of customer satisfaction at

FIGURE 2

Performance drivers for a consumer retail bank

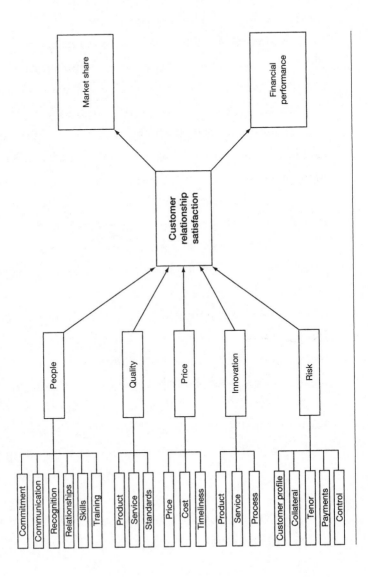

Citibank. It allows us to understand why this measure is so important to division executives. But it also raises questions. Are any variables missing? Are any specified incorrectly? Are the linkages correct?

Your theory of value creation need not be this complex. A simple theory is easier to communicate. For example, CEO Bill Marriott's theory is widely understood within Marriott's twenty-five hundred hotels: "If your employees are well taken care of, they'll take care of the customer and the customer will come back. That's basically the core value of the company."[2]

Marriott's value-creation theory has been repeated so many times that everyone understands the reason for management's focus on four critical performance measures: associate satisfaction, guest satisfaction, revenue, and RevPAR (revenue per available room). Marriott uses these measures for setting goals and evaluating managers. It tracks them carefully so it can link them to bonuses and promotions. There is no uncertainty. Everyone knows what he or she is accountable for and acts accordingly.

What Is Your Theory of Value Creation?

What is your theory of value creation? Can you state it in a few simple sentences or does it require a more complicated diagram? Regardless of its form, your job is to clarify your business strategy so that everyone can understand it and focus his or her efforts on the variables that are critical to value creation.

IDENTIFYING WHAT'S TRULY CRITICAL

If your theory of value creation is at all complex—like the consumer bank diagram—people will still need help figuring out which variables are truly critical. Tough choices must be made.

Look back at the performance drivers for the consumer bank. There are twenty-eight variables in this diagram. Which are truly critical? Does "recognition" carry the same weight as "risk"? How about "cost" and "communication"? Which is more important?

You have probably seen scorecards with thirty, forty, fifty, even sixty measures, created with the mistaken belief that adding more measures to a scorecard results in a more complete—and therefore better—scorecard. Information technology has evolved to a point that we can measure more and more things at lower and lower cost. So why not add more measures?

The reason is simple, but often overlooked: management attention is your scarcest resource. As you add more and more measures to your scorecards, you pay an opportunity cost. People have less time to focus on what really matters. The truly critical variables become lost in an overload of extraneous measures.

It's easy to understand how this can happen. In many organizations, executives want to be inclusive—to signal to everyone that their work is valued. So they dutifully include measures and metrics for every role and function to ensure that no one feels excluded. But in doing so, they confuse "nice to have" with "critical." Dilution of attention and loss of focus are the inevitable outcome. And so is underperformance.

It's your job to simplify. Larry Bossidy, retired head of Honeywell, reminds us, "A leader who says, 'I've got ten priorities' doesn't know what he's talking about—he doesn't know himself what the most important things are . . . Leaders who execute well focus on a very few clear priorities that everyone can grasp. You've got to have these few, clearly realistic goals and priorities, which will influence the overall performance of the company.[3] . . . I usually try to select only three key measures in any one year, depending on the times. I don't think you have to measure the same thing all of the time."[4]

There's also another problem to consider. As you add more variables and measures to your scorecards, you will inevitably drive out innovation. In the old McDonald's—the one that focused on franchise growth and standardized food—field consultants visited each store quarterly to measure compliance with prescribed operating standards. They analyzed and reported on over five hundred metrics in a twenty-five-page report. Because of the constraints these measures imposed, store managers had no freedom whatsoever in how they operated their restaurants. There was no opportunity to innovate or to respond to consumer preferences. Standardized mediocrity—driven by an overload of measures—was the result.[5]

Any scorecard that has too many measures will cause a similar problem. An overload of measures will reduce degrees of freedom and dictate how people should do their jobs. They are forced to operate in a straitjacket. And if they are overloaded with measures that are merely nice to have, you can bet that they will be feeling overwhelmed and frustrated.

If you think it's time to simplify your scorecards, here's a technique to help you decide which measures to keep and which to discard.

FOCUS ON FAILURE

Picture yourself five or seven years from now. Instead of envisioning success, imagine the worst. Envision a scene in which your strategy has failed: your products have lost their edge, your competitors have overtaken you, your best people have left. Imagine that your strategy is in ruins.

What could have gone wrong? What could have caused this disaster?

This is an unpleasant exercise, but necessary for identifying the performance variables so critical to your strategy that, if your business failed on these dimensions, you could see your entire strategy failing.

Although a focus on failure may seem extreme, it's a technique Warren Buffett uses extensively. His advice: "Invert, always invert. Turn a situation or problem upside down. Look at it backward . . . What happens if all our plans go wrong? Where don't we want to go and how do we get there? Instead of looking for success, make a list of how you can fail instead."[6]

What Could Cause Your Strategy to Fail?

What could cause your strategy to fail? Is it the inability to leverage new technology? Supply of low-cost components? Quality? Relationships with government officials? Attracting good people?

Each strategy is different, but you should be able to list three things that are so important to your company's success that, if your business fails on these variables, your entire strategy may be at risk. What would they be? Take a moment to write them down:

1. _____

2. _____

3. _____

These critical variables should be at the very top of the things that you, and your management team, track and monitor. Are they? Or are they lost in a long list of measures that are of relatively little importance.

This exercise raises questions. For example, an imagined failure of Citibank's strategy—with its focus on relationship banking—may depend more on customer loyalty than on customer satisfaction. Building long-term relationships with target segment customers is the critical underpinning of the strategy, not attempting to satisfy customers who come to the bank to conduct routine passbook transactions.

Every organization has only a handful of measures that are truly critical to the successful implementation of its strategy. At Amazon, convenience for buyers tops the list of things that could cause its strategy to fail. So executives focus on making purchasing as easy as possible and focus their attention on revenue per click and revenue per page turn.[7] At Citibank, it's customer satisfaction (or perhaps customer loyalty), coupled with market share and revenue from targeted customers. At Marriott, the focus is on associate satisfaction, guest satisfaction, and two financial measures: revenue and RevPar.

Even after you've identified critical performance variables, choosing the right measures for your business may take some ingenuity. To illustrate, consider retailer Nordstrom. Its high-service, full-price strategy depends on the continuing loyalty of its upscale customers. Surprisingly, it doesn't attempt to measure customer loyalty directly. Instead, it relies on the measurement of its associates' sales per hour. This may seem like an odd choice, but it's based on a clear understanding of what it takes to execute strategy successfully in this business.

Nordstrom executives believe that hiring and retaining sales associates capable of building customer loyalty is the most critical ingredient of their strategy. They have learned that the best salespeople treat their customers as assets: keeping records of customers' sizes and style preferences, calling up their customers when new items come into the store, and offering to make personal deliveries to ease the purchasing experience. Because of this high commitment to service, the best sales associates generate high levels of customer loyalty, high repeat sales, and high sales per hour. By contrast, people who don't have the energy or initiative to offer such levels of service suffer low sales-per-hour scores and eventually leave the company.[8]

Are your scorecards streamlined to focus on the critical few measures that truly strike at the heart of your strategy execution? Or are they cluttered with too many variables that don't really matter, variables that are nice to have, but don't define the difference between success and failure.

HOW MANY MEASURES?

Managers often have difficulty deciding how many measures to hold someone accountable for. This is one area where I can provide an easy answer: seven, plus or minus two.[9]

The idea is simple. People can remember seven things (and as many as nine, in a pinch). If they can easily recall the measures they're accountable for, the measures will influence the choices they make as they go about their work. This is simple to test. Ask someone who works for you what measures he's accountable for. If his score-card has fifteen or twenty-five or forty measures, he will not be able to recall them, and the measures will have minimal impact on his day-to-day behavior. If he's accountable for seven measures (plus or minus two), he'll have no trouble remembering them—and consistently pursuing those goals.

Why the lower bound? Why no fewer than five? Because with too few measures, there's not enough variety to stimulate creativity. The multiple perspectives and trade-offs generated by at least five measures—and preferably seven—will often foster new ideas and new ways of approaching problems (I will have more to say on this in chapter 5).

How universally can you apply this rule? Think of all the things in our lives configured in sevens: days of the week, notes on the musical scale, colors in the rainbow, wonders of the world, deadly sins, habits of highly effective people (not to mention Snow White's dwarfs). The seven digits of telephone numbers also fell in the easy-to-remember category until area codes were added. (But if you're like me, you stopped trying to memorize telephone numbers when that happened and instead now store them in the memory of your mobile phone.)

How about the seven strategy questions? My hope is that you—and others in your business—can easily remember them so that you can ask these questions regularly to help you execute your strategy better.

FINANCIAL PERFORMANCE MEASURES

Once you're confident that you have identified the right strategic variables—and the measures to track them—you still need to be sure that you are tracking the right financial measures. It's easy to get caught up with the glamour of strategic scorecards and ignore the fundamentals.

The financial variables you should be tracking are illustrated in three interlocking profit wheels, shown in figure 3.[10]

Start with the center wheel. Almost all companies hold managers accountable for sales revenue, operating expenses, net income, and investment in assets. But this is the bare minimum. Managers are often surprised how much additional funds can be freed up for strategic

FIGURE 3

Profit wheels

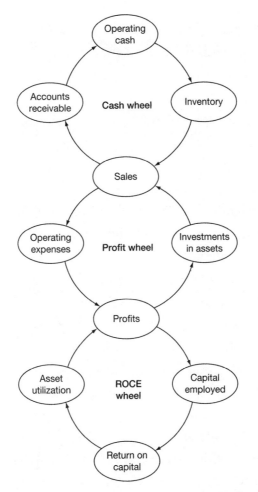

initiatives if they manage their working capital effectively. So, better companies also track measures in the top wheel: accounts receivable, operating cash, and inventory. The best companies add, in addition, measures in the lower wheel for return on capital employed (ROCE)—balance sheet assets, return on capital, and asset utilization. These companies expect managers to leverage all company assets effectively to optimize financial performance.

High-performing companies recognize that such financial measures are always critical to success. Consider Apple, a company known for its innovative product designs and industry-leading technology. The company also emphasizes inventory turns, cash flow management, and balance-sheet asset accounts. In a business where obsolescence can decrease the value of unsold goods by as much as 2 percent per week, COO Tim Cook has argued that inventory is "fundamentally evil." Apple executives have reduced inventory turnover to days instead of months. Cook elaborates, "You want to manage inventory like you're in the dairy business. If it gets past its freshness date, you have a problem."[11]

The flip side of this coin is that any company with inadequate financial controls should immediately be suspect. Good financial systems are a prerequisite for good management.

AIG's rise to industry prominence was imperiously managed by CEO Hank Greenberg, who, in 2009, paid

$15 million in fines for overseeing fraudulent accounting transactions.[12] Even with Greenberg out of the picture, the notoriously inefficient system, with its lack of checks and balances, has proved to be a major stumbling block for the executives who followed. After massive federal bailouts, AIG vice chairman Paula Reynolds stated, "The best businesses are run by people who kick the tires every day. We don't even know where the tires are, much less get to kick them."[13]

Is your financial system up to the task of supporting your strategy? At a minimum, you should be holding managers accountable for revenue, expenses, and profit margins. If you want to do more than the bare minimum, add accountability for cash flow measures to ensure that you are managing working capital efficiently. If you want to be in the best-practices camp, you should be holding your managers accountable not only for profit and cash flow, but also for balance sheet ROCE measures to ensure that all assets are managed effectively.

How does your business measure up?

CREATING ACCOUNTABILITY

Once you've identified the right critical performance variables—both financial and nonfinancial—and eliminated the distractions, you must embed them in a broader system of goal setting, accountability, and rewards. In other words, they must be linked to consequences.

One of the criticisms leveled against former GM CEO Rick Wagoner—who is widely admired as a decent and caring executive—was that he was too forgiving. Although the company lost more than $70 billion in four years, Wagoner fired virtually no executives for inadequate performance. He allowed weak divisions and dealerships to continue in the face of year-after-year poor performance.[14]

JPMorgan Chase's CEO Jamie Dimon follows a different approach. He demands strict accountability. A subordinate recounted, "He's a demanding boss and when he is unhappy with your performance he lets you know it. He runs a culture of accountability that keeps everyone on their toes."[15] To reinforce this message, Dimon instituted a system that ranks branch managers based on their revenue and profit contribution. Top performers receive bonuses up to $65,000, while those in the lowest quintile get nothing.[16]

How Do You Create Accountability for Performance?

How do you create accountability for performance in your business? The most common approach is to link compensation to performance. But compensation is not the only way to get people to pay attention. Your own attention and follow-up will also get the job done.

Procter & Gamble's A. G. Lafley described how, when he took over as CEO, he inherited a company with too many initiatives and poor profitability. His solution was simple: build personal accountability. When he discovered that sales were suffering because some products were not available for immediate shipment, Lafley required subordinates to report the number of missed cases to him weekly. "Every Monday morning, my leadership team was asked to report to me on missed cases and what actions were taken to fill orders. We continued the practice until missed cases were in much better control. Today, missed cases run less than 0.4 percent, and they are no longer a major cause of lost sales and profits."[17]

Building accountability for critical performance measures was also the approach Frank Blake adopted when he took over as CEO of Home Depot. Previous CEO Bob Nardelli had instituted scorecards with fifteen pages of detailed measures. Not surprisingly, store managers complained of a bewildering array of metrics. Blake remedied this situation by reducing the number of critical measures to eight (with customer satisfaction at the top of the list) and holding store managers personally accountable for performance against those measures.[18]

You may be wondering what happened to James McGaran at Citibank. Johnson and Reiger scored McGaran below par on the customer satisfaction measure. But they gave him an overall above-par rating, even though the scorecard rules said that this was not permissible. His bonus was reduced by a modest 5 percent. Reiger said that he wanted to recognize the good job that McGaran had done and did not want to risk losing him. But he also wanted to signal—to McGaran and the rest of the organization—the importance of customer satisfaction as a critical performance variable.

What do you think of their decision?

TRACKING PERFORMANCE GOALS

This chapter is the first of two intended to test your success in focusing everyone in your business on your strategic agenda.

In many organizations, people feel overwhelmed with too many initiatives and too many measures. It's your job is to cut through this clutter by clarifying your theory of value creation, identifying what could cause your strategy to fail, and focusing on a few truly *critical* performance measures that will lead to success.

Have you satisfied this imperative?

If so, it's time to move on to the next chapter, where we explore how you can set strategic boundaries to further enhance focus and, at the same time, protect your most critical asset: your company's reputation.

FOUR

WHAT STRATEGIC BOUNDARIES HAVE YOU SET?

In 1996, CEO John Seffrin proposed ambitious goals for the American Cancer Society. By 2015, he declared, the number of cancer death rates would fall by half and the number of people diagnosed with the disease would be reduced by a quarter. Results to date have been encouraging. With improved prevention and therapy, cancer mortality rates have declined steadily. Between 2002 and 2004, for example, cancer death rates declined more than 2 percent per year.

But by 2006, there was still a long way to go. The biggest impediment was access to health care. Research showed a strong correlation between cancer survival rates and health insurance coverage. For example, a woman with stage I breast cancer but no insurance was more likely to die than a woman with more serious stage II cancer who had insurance. So in 2006, the American Cancer Society announced a new "Access to Care" strategy. The society would attempt to sway public opinion through advocacy. Working closely with primary physicians, it would promote wider access to health care by educating the society's 3 million volunteers and lobbying state and federal legislators.

The new strategy created grave risks. The society's annual revenue came from 15 million donors who each gave an average of $75. As Seffrin acknowledged, "Ninety-seven percent of our gross receipts come from individual donors. So, if people don't like what we're doing, they just stop giving."[1]

Seffrin worried that donors might misconstrue Access to Care as a call for socialized medicine or a single-payer system, concepts which many Americans opposed. To protect against this risk, he stated explicitly that the society would not lobby for a single-payer health system and decreed the following boundaries for each of the society's eight thousand employees:

We will not be partisan.

We will not endorse or oppose the platforms of particular political candidates.

We will not give money to political candidates.

We will not form or support political action committees.[2]

The society would work to unite both liberals and conservatives in the fight against cancer, but it would not represent a particular political point of view. To do so would alienate a large portion of its donor base and imperil its mission.

These "do nots" may seem out of place in an organization whose mission is to eliminate cancer. But they were essential to the successful execution of the new strategy.

Every organization—including yours—must face the risk that employees may make choices or act in ways that could damage its strategy. Have you inoculated your business against this risk?

Controlling strategic risk is the fourth implementation imperative. This is an important sequel to the previous chapter on critical performance variables for two reasons. First, pressures created by performance goals may encourage some individuals to act in ways that could jeopardize your business strategy. For example, they may feel pressure to cut quality to hit growth targets. You must protect against this risk. Second, if people are to execute your strategic agenda successfully, you must ensure that they are not wasting effort and resources on initiatives that do not align with your desired direction for the business. Setting boundaries is a critical tool to accomplish both these objectives.

THE POWER OF NEGATIVE THINKING

There are two ways to control risk: you can tell people what to do, or tell them what not to do.

Telling people what to do provides assurance that they won't make mistakes or engage in unauthorized activities. They will do what they're told and nothing else. This is the prudent approach if safety and quality are paramount concerns—say, if you're running a nuclear power plant or overseeing a space launch. In such cases, you want to limit discretion by requiring employees to follow standard operating procedures to the letter. The last thing you want is for plant operators and technicians to experiment by taking unauthorized risks.

However, if innovation and entrepreneurial thinking are important to your business strategy, specifying exactly how everyone should do his or her job is not a desirable approach. Instead, you should hire talented and creative people—the best you can find—and then tell them what *not* to do. This provides the freedom to exercise their creativity within defined limits.

This is an old idea. Take, for example, the Ten Commandments. The commandments don't tell readers what to do, but rather what not to do ("Thou shall not . . .").

We pay attention to these prohibitions because they are enforced by threat of punishment, not rewards for good behavior.

All leaders can utilize the power of negative thinking. Hire people with passion, inspire them, and give them aggressive goals and incentives. But also tell them what behaviors will get them fired.

You should always state boundaries in the negative. This has three benefits. First, telling people what not to do provides absolute clarity about where you have drawn the line in the sand. There is no ambiguity. Second, people pay more attention when you tell them what will get them fired than when you tell them about your lofty new vision and strategy. Finally, defining what is unacceptable gives them freedom to act without constant uncertainty and worry that you might later judge their actions as inappropriate.

If you have a code of business conduct, you already have basic boundaries in place. Such documents typically prohibit illegal activities such as insider trading and other breaches of corporate integrity. But most employees don't pay much attention to these codes of conduct. They probably haven't even read them in detail. Why not? Because too often the "do nots" are hidden in a thicket of prose that muddles the message.

If your code of conduct is more than a couple of pages long, you have fallen victim to misguided attempts to mix inspiration with "thou shall nots." The Ten

Commandments are concise for good reason. Boundaries have only one purpose: to tell people what not to do. Boundaries should specify the behaviors that are unacceptable in your business and will not be tolerated under any circumstance. This is not the place to inspire with your mission, values, and strategy.

You can use the power of negative thinking—the foundation for every code of business conduct—to develop boundaries that will help you execute your strategy effectively. As in previous chapters, we again focus on an adjective to pose the next question—What strategic boundaries have you set?

What Strategic Boundaries Have You Set?

Strategic boundaries are similar to codes of conduct, with one exception. They are tailored to the specific strategic risks of your business.

There are two kinds of risks that strategic boundaries protect against: (1) the possibility that people will engage in behaviors that could damage your company's reputation, and (2) the risk that resources will be diverted to opportunities that don't align with your current strategy.

PROTECTING YOUR REPUTATION

Certain actions and behaviors by a corporation or its employees, if reported publicly, can fatally erode the confidence of your customers and constituents. At the beginning of this chapter, I described the boundaries that American Cancer Society executives put in place to ensure donors would not interpret their new Access to Care strategy as an endorsement of a particular political point of view. There was good reason for their precaution. When President Obama announced publicly that the AARP supported an early version of his health care reform bill, the organization lost more than fifty thousand members in two months. Those who quit objected on either philosophical grounds or fears that the proposal would cut their Medicare coverage.[3]

Some people call this franchise risk. Others use the term reputation or headline risk. But the idea is the same—a loss of confidence by customers, suppliers, regulators, or investors can sink your entire strategy.

During the global financial crisis, we were all reminded that the consequences of lost confidence can be swift and irrevocable. Executives at Bear Sterns and Lehman Brothers were unable to recover when lenders began to worry about the ability of these firms to survive. As Bear Sterns veered into increasingly risky mortgage origination and securitization businesses, counterparties grew nervous. In the end, lenders declined to finance the $50 billion overnight float that Bear needed to keep its business solvent. As one analyst noted, "Bear's reliance on overnight repurchasing agreements effectively gave lenders such as Fidelity and Federated Investors a vote on the firm's viability every night."[4] The company soon declared bankruptcy.

A similar reputation loss occurred at Citigroup when regulators discovered that bank employees in Japan were helping clients generate illegal transactions to hide losses. Japanese regulators forced Citigroup to close its private banking business, and the company was later forced to shutter its investment management and real estate advisory businesses. The photograph of CEO Chuck Prince bowing deeply in apology at a Tokyo news conference, reproduced on the front pages of financial newspapers around the world, was a chilling reminder of the consequences of reputation risk.[5]

This and other Citigroup infractions—including dealings with WorldCom, Global Crossing, and Enron—caused the U.S. Federal Reserve to issue a ban on all Citigroup expansion or acquisitions until the company improved its compliance controls. A chastened Citigroup executive explained, "We always thought doing business the right way was what the organization does. We thought saying 'don't do anything stupid, don't do anything illegal' was a given. Maybe it wasn't."[6]

Citigroup is not alone. Many business leaders learn the importance of setting boundaries only after a reputational crisis imperils their business. At General Electric, an unexpected crisis erupted when two junior engineers were accused of shifting costs from a fixed-price contract to a cost-plus contract on a defense contract. The consequences of the accusations were swift and severe. GE was suspended as a supplier to the entire U.S. government, putting over $4 billion in annual revenue at risk.

CEO Jack Welch acted quickly to create Policy 20.10—a one-page document that listed the behaviors that were prohibited when doing work for the U.S. government. At the top of the list was mischarging costs. Policy 20.10 also spelled out the consequences for misdeeds: GE would fire individuals and their managers for violations.[7]

What are your major reputation risks? You—and every business leader—must live with the knowledge that someone, somewhere, might do something that could damage your company's reputation. To guard against this risk, you must eliminate any uncertainty about what is unacceptable and declare those activities off-limits. You should be especially vigilant about the possibility that people might take unacceptable risks to hit their performance targets—especially when growth and profit goals are being pushed aggressively.

What Are Your Major Reputation Risks?

At Toyota—long recognized as a leader in automotive quality—employees cut quality standards in their quest to overtake GM as worldwide sales leader. To encourage faster growth, the company abandoned a strategic boundary that had safeguarded its quality reputation for decades. It was a simple rule: never build a new product in a new factory with a new workforce. Toyota ignored this strategic boundary—which ensured that best-quality methods would be transferred from factory to factory—in 2006 when it began building its new Tundra at a brand-new plant in Texas with a new workforce. It made similar decisions to cut corners around the world in the race to be number one. But there was a price to be paid. In 2010, the company was forced to recall 8 million vehicles, stop the sale of its most popular car models, and halt production in five North American plants to fix quality problems. Toyota's reputation—the basis of its successful market franchise—was severely damaged.[8]

Your strategy—and the industry in which you compete—will determine the type of boundaries that are needed to protect your reputation. Only you can decide what's right for your business. To illustrate the range of possibilities, here are some examples from firms in four different industries: retail, consulting, information technology, and health care.

In the retail business, Walmart has a strict boundary that forbids executives from accepting gifts and favors—even a cup of coffee from a supplier. The company has gone so far as to terminate a vice president for accepting free meals.[9] Why such harsh treatment? Executives believe this prohibition is necessary to avoid preferential treatment to suppliers that could impair Walmart's low-cost strategy.

In consulting, McKinsey has a strict code of conduct that forbids employees from disclosing information about a client to anyone—even a spouse.[10] McKinsey immediately terminates anyone caught breaking this client confidentiality rule. There is good reason for this paranoia. McKinsey was severely embarrassed in 2009 when a senior partner was arrested for leaking information about the acquisition plans of clients to a hedge fund. This incident, widely reported in the financial press, put McKinsey's entire business at risk. Its franchise relies on the willingness of clients to entrust proprietary strategic data to McKinsey consultants. It terminated the partner involved, but not before serious damage had been done to the firm's reputation.[11]

In the information technology industry, Google's leadership position in the search business is wholly dependent on its reputation for independence. If users believe that advertisers who pay to appear on the Google site bias search results, they can switch instantly and without cost to competing search engines. Because of this strategic risk, Google has published clear boundaries for its employees: "No short-term gain could ever justify breaching our users' trust. There can be no compromising of the integrity of our results. We never manipulate rankings to put our partners higher in our search results. No one can buy a better PageRank."[12]

Halfway around the world in a completely different industry, Sydney IVF, an Australian in vitro fertilization business, has created strategic boundaries to ensure that the company maintains the trust of couples who use their clinics to conceive a baby. Sydney IVF will not allow:

- Anonymous egg or sperm donations (due to every child's right to know his or her genetic heritage)

- Embryo donations to other couples (due to the potential for psychological trauma when people learn later in life that they have genetic siblings in another family)

- Cloning (due to risks of producing genetically unhealthy individuals)

- Sex selection (due to legal restrictions)[13]

Each of these examples is very different: from the American Cancer Society to Toyota to Sydney IVF to Walmart, McKinsey, and Google. Different industries, different customers, different strategies. But the implication is the same across the board. If reputation is a key asset for the execution of your strategy, you should create clear strategic boundaries that leave no doubt as to what behaviors are unacceptable—and the consequences for those who step over the line.

Does everyone in your business know what actions are off-limits? If not, your entire strategy—as good as it may be—could one day be put in jeopardy.

Does Everyone Know What Actions Are Off-Limits?

OPPORTUNITIES TO AVOID

The second type of strategic boundary—again drawing on the power of negative thinking—stipulates what projects and business opportunities to avoid. This type of strategic boundary is intended to make everyone focus on your strategic agenda.

In any business with creative people, new ideas will abound. People will innovate and pursue new opportunities, especially if you are using the performance goals described in chapter 3 (and the techniques to spur innovation discussed in chapter 5). But unbridled creativity and unfocused initiatives can pull your strategy off course. People will be working in too many different directions and wasting scarce resources, resources that should be devoted to executing your current agenda.

Undisciplined growth usually spells trouble. This risk was clear in hindsight to Starbucks' founder Howard Schultz. He lamented that the rapid expansion from one thousand to seventeen thousand stores diluted the Starbucks brand (the company opened over twenty-five hundred new stores in 2007 alone).[14] Describing the uncontrolled expansion into dreary strip malls, he recalled, "We did not have the discipline to say no. The issue was our failure to say, 'That store in that location should not be opened.'"[15]

Strategic boundaries avoid the waste and frustration that is inevitable with undisciplined growth. Managers find nothing so frustrating as investing time and resources in what they think is an innovative and worthy project only to learn at the last minute that senior executives won't support it. Strategic boundaries can avoid this wasted effort by focusing entrepreneurial energy. Instead of telling people what to do—and thereby limiting their creativity—tell managers in advance what strategic initiatives to avoid.

Steve Jobs claims that, without the discipline to say no to pressures to develop PDAs, Apple would not have had sufficient resources to develop the iPod. Says Jobs, "People think focus means saying yes to the things you've got to focus on. But that's not what it means at all. It means saying no to the one hundred other good ideas."[16]

To have a clear strategy, tough choices are necessary. Strategic boundaries at brokerage firm Edward Jones spell out exactly what it will not do: "We do not sell penny stocks, commodities, or other high-risk instruments. We do not serve day traders and see no need to offer online trading . . . We do not advise institutions or companies . . .

We do not offer services such as checking accounts for their own sake . . . We do not target self-directed do-it-yourselfers."[17]

No matter what the nature of your business, you should be able to state which opportunities you will leave on the table for others. Why? Because trying to be everything to everyone in every market can mean only one thing: you don't have a clear strategy.

The idea of setting strategic boundaries is not new. It was the basis of General Motors's original business strategy. To segment multiple product offerings, Alfred Sloan assigned each operating company a price range within which its products must compete. He did not say what price point vehicles should be sold for, but he did dictate the prices they could not be sold for: the upper and lower prices for each brand.[18] One hundred years later, GM had forgotten this important lesson. Its portfolio of American brands—Chevrolet, Oldsmobile, Buick, Pontiac, Saturn—had such overlap that it was impossible to create distinctive market positions.

Saying no to a profitable project or new opportunity is never popular. There is often pressure to eliminate strategic boundaries, especially when you are offered profitable opportunities that don't quite fit the current strategic agenda. Here's an example. When energy giant AES was founded, executives created a ceiling on investments in a single market to ensure that no one overinvested in developing countries. They originally set this boundary at 5 percent of cash flow and invested capital. In the 1990s, they raised the limit to 10 percent. Then in the late 1990s, when new opportunities came along at an increasing rate, executives decided to eliminate the boundary altogether. Founder Dennis Bakke, who left the company as it teetered on the edge of bankruptcy, later described this as an act of arrogance that dramatically increased the huge losses and write-offs that would follow.[19]

Even if not popular, saying no is good business. Wells Fargo executives weathered the 2008 to 2009 financial crisis—and earned the admiration of Warren Buffett—because they set boundaries that told employees to avoid structured investment products and low-documentation mortgage loans. Unlike most of its competitors, Wells Fargo also refused to lend money at below-market rates to Berkshire Hathaway in hopes of earning Buffett's future business. This refusal won Buffett's respect. He stated with a laugh, "I got a big kick out of that because that's exactly how they should think. The real insight you get about a banker is . . . what they don't do. And what Wells didn't do defines its greatness."[20]

Strategic boundaries can take many forms. You can (and should) specify projects to avoid, products to avoid, markets to avoid, and so on. What strategic initiatives will you *not* support?

One of my favorite examples of strategic boundaries—and strategic clarity—is ADP, the payroll-processing company. ADPs strategic boundaries state that it will not support any business that cannot:

What Strategic Initiatives Will You *Not* Support?

- Generate $100 million in recurring annual revenue.

- Sustain a 15 percent growth rate.

- Be number one or two in its market, with the potential to be number one in five years.

- Offer standardized noncustomized products and services.

- Have a clear exit plan.

These boundaries are not a straitjacket. Executives revisit them every three years to confirm that they are still appropriate—and adjust them if necessary. And they will still allocate limited resources for projects that do not meet all these requirements. But every business must conform over a relatively short period of time or it's divested. The clarity these boundaries provide has constrained growth—ADP is not as big as it might otherwise be—but it has also allowed the company to be consistently profitable, with the longest run of unbroken double-digit earnings-per-share increases of any publicly traded U.S. company.[21] As of January 2010, ADP was also one of only four nonfinancial companies that held a triple-A credit rating (the others were Exxon, Microsoft, and Johnson & Johnson).[22]

Every company—even one that thrives on chaos—needs strategic boundaries. Consider Google, a company known for its "disorderly conduct." Executives encourage engineers to spend 20 percent of their time on projects outside their main area of responsibility.[23] But they quickly kill experimental projects if they fail to meet four hurdles: the project must be popular with customers; sponsors must be able to attract other employees to work on it; the project must solve big problems; and it must meet internal performance targets. These boundaries—which allow freedom by clarifying the projects that will *not* be supported—limit the time that is wasted on projects that are unlikely to have a strategic future.[24]

Do your employees know what strategic initiatives you will not support? If not, you need more clarity in your strategic thinking.

PUTTING WORDS INTO ACTION

Your decision to use—or not use—boundaries to manage risk will affect the type of people your business will attract. Some people want to work for organizations where they're told exactly how to do their jobs. They are comfortable—in fact, prefer—following orders. The organization that attracts such people will lack creativity, spontaneity, and innovation. But it's exactly the right fit for some.

Individuals with energy and entrepreneurial spirit will choose an entirely different kind of business. These people value freedom above all else. Their favored employer will be the company that doesn't tell them what to do, but instead tells them what not to do. And then gives them the freedom to act to the best of their abilities within those constraints.

Boundaries are the antithesis of bureaucracy, with its rules, manuals, and standard operating procedures. By design, boundaries are short, but not sweet. Whether it's risk to your reputation or the risk of diverting resources, you should be able to write your boundaries on the back of a napkin. You don't need to hire consultants or high-powered staff specialists to do this. Based on your knowledge of your business and its strategy, you should be able to state—in no more than a page—what activities are off-limits.

But if you choose to set boundaries, you must remember that they are powered by punishment, not rewards. Therefore, you must be willing to discipline—and fire, if necessary—anyone caught stepping over the line. By following up forcefully and consistently, word of your actions will travel throughout your organization, reinforcing the importance of the prohibitions that you have stipulated.

These are tough—but necessary—decisions. And they are nowhere more important than at the top. If you think that this could never happen to you—that no one in your company would ever do something to put your franchise at risk—think again. People are fallible. Transgressions are inevitable. But many companies don't have the courage to follow through. They don't want to shine a light on, or admit, the fact that someone has acted inappropriately.

Johnson & Johnson, a company well known for its credo and values, does have such courage. When it discovered that managers in a foreign subsidiary had bribed officials to secure sales of its medical devices—a practice outlawed by its code of conduct and the Foreign Corrupt Practices Act—it immediately informed the SEC and U.S. Justice Department. It fired the managers involved. More important from the perspective of corporate integrity, the worldwide chairman of J&J's medical devices division—who was not directly implicated—accepted ultimate responsibility and resigned.[25]

CONTROLLING STRATEGIC RISK

Boundaries leverage the power of negative thinking to create freedom. People want to know where your boundaries are, so they can understand the activities that are off-limits and the type of initiatives you do not support.

With clear *strategic* boundaries, everyone is free to exercise his or her full creative potential in support of your strategy. In combination with the critical performance variables discussed in the previous chapter, strategic boundaries focus everyone on your strategic agenda.

Have you satisfied this imperative? Have you made the tough choices about what people should *not* do? If not, your strategic agenda is at risk.

If you feel you have this imperative under control, you're ready to move on to the next topic: how to motivate all the people in your business to stretch themselves to win. This is the subject of the next chapter, where I will ask you to make some additional tough choices. But you shouldn't turn the page unless you are confident that your boundaries are sufficiently strong to protect your organization from the pressures you are about to create.

FIVE

HOW ARE YOU GENERATING CREATIVE TENSION?

Rod and Bob Johnstone, founders of J Boats, were worried. The boat-building industry was in a tailspin, and the survival of their business was in jeopardy.

On November 5, 1990, President George H. W. Bush had signed a new tax bill, famously breaking his pledge, "Read my lips: No new taxes." Starting January 1, a 10 percent luxury tax was to be levied on jewelry and furs costing more than $10,000, cars valued above $30,000, boats costing more than $100,000, and recreational aircraft above $250,000.[1]

The effects on the boat industry were devastating. A prominent New York dealer, who had sold thirty luxury boats the prior year, sold only two in 1991. Yacht sales across the country dropped 77 percent. Twenty-five thousand workers had been laid off, and boatbuilders were declaring bankruptcy.[2] Rod and Bob knew that if they didn't come up with something new, they could be next.

The story of J Boats was a legend in the boating industry. Like Hewlett-Packard founders Bill Hewitt and David Packard, who built their first products in a modest garage in Palo Alto, Rod Johnstone had built his prototype J/24 sailboat in his Connecticut garage. Rod explained, "The garage was twenty-eight feet long with a workbench at one end, and the door was nine feet wide. It was no accident that the boat was twenty-four feet by eight feet, eleven inches." The J/24, launched in 1976, would become the most famous and widely recognized sailboat in the world. Over the ensuing years, the company built thousands of boats and expanded its line to include models from twenty-two feet to fifty-two feet. More than a hundred thousand people around the world sailed J boats each year. *Fortune* magazine hailed J Boats as one of the one hundred best products manufactured in America.

In the spring of 1991, a crisis loomed. In response to dying demand, Bob Johnstone prepared a concept proposal for an entirely new type of sailboat that could be built by their company. It must cost less than $100,000 to avoid the luxury tax; be fast, fun, and easy to sail; and leverage J Boats' reputation for performance and quality.

The thirty-five foot boat that designer Rod Johnstone created in response—the J/105—was a hit. The streamlined "sportboat" concept, with its retractable bowsprit, pumped new life into J Boats and led to a revolution in the industry as competitors followed suit. Today, J Boats remains the leader in its high-performance, high-quality niche.

Without the pressure of the luxury tax (which was repealed in 1993), this industry-leading innovation might never have been conceived. Bob Johnstone attributed the idea to what he called, "the cornered rat theory of creativity." When pushed to the wall, you must innovate or die.[3]

MARKET PRESSURES TO INNOVATE

Entrepreneurs, and those who work in entrepreneurial start-ups, know what it's like to feel pressure to innovate. They must find ways to deliver products and services valued by customers or die. There is no choice. The marketplace is an impartial and unsympathetic judge of competitive success.

If you shield people in your business from such competitive pressures, they are unlikely to innovate. And the bigger your organization, the more people can comfortably hide from the pressures of external competition. As a senior HR executive complained, "Historically, winning for our people has been getting to the next job grade faster than anyone else, rather than winning in the marketplace."

No matter what the nature of your business—large or small—if you operate in competitive markets, you must innovate constantly to stay ahead of the game. Some innovations may be incremental improvements. Others may be breakthrough. But if you don't innovate, someone else will—taking your customers with them. On the flip side, shielding companies from competition—whether through monopoly regulation or government protectionist policies—is a sure recipe for stagnation of new ideas and the artificial support of businesses that are unsustainable in the long run.

Techniques for encouraging innovation in larger organizations are well known. Autonomous teams, virtual networks, and resources for skunk-work experimentation are just some of the ways that you can create innovation-friendly environments. While these techniques are useful in creating favorable conditions for innovation, they are not enough. They tell you how to lead the horse to water, but they don't take the final—and crucial—step. They don't tell you how to get it to drink.

In this chapter, we look at techniques for *spurring innovation*—the fifth implementation imperative. Rather than just creating favorable conditions and hoping for the best, are you doing enough to push people to their creative limits? I have chosen the verb *spurring* deliberately. The techniques we will consider have a hard edge to them. They are uncomfortable, but essential, if you want to achieve high levels of innovation and performance.

I realize that I'm stepping into dangerous territory here. Putting pressure on people for performance brings risk, especially if done carelessly. (Before applying these techniques, you should be sure that you have prioritized your core values, communicated minimum responsibility to others, and set clear strategic boundaries.) But not applying pressure brings even more risk—a failure to innovate that can, over time, sap your company of its competitive edge.

The next question—How are you generating creative tension?—will test to see if you are using the right techniques to maximize innovation in your business.

Innovation occurs naturally in competitive markets. But it doesn't occur naturally inside organizations. We all fall into predictable routines and habits. How many of

How Are You Generating Creative Tension?

us have experienced the sensation when, lost deep in thought, we realize that we have driven several miles on our way to work without the slightest recollection of the journey? Our work routines provide the same kind of mindless response. We do the same things day in and day out in ways that are similar to what we've done before.

To spur innovation, you must break these comfortable habits. You must push people out of their comfort zones by infusing your business with creative tension. Of course, not everyone can rise to this challenge. Creative ability varies across individuals. But I guarantee that if you do not put pressure on people to innovate to the best of their abilities—as uncomfortable as this may seem— they will remain stuck in predictable routines. And the risks will rise that your business will be left behind as more innovative competitors leap ahead.

CREATING PRESSURE TO WIN

Most businesses are not entrepreneurial start-ups facing life or death market pressures. But executives of all businesses can mimic the same approaches.

As a business leader, one of your primary jobs is to import market pressures inside your business—to motivate people to think and act like competitors. And like any competition, the goal is to win. Andy Grove, former CEO of Intel, underlined the importance of this point: "The most important role of managers is to create an environment in which people are passionately dedicated to winning in the marketplace."[4]

Only you can decide how much innovation your company needs to support your strategy and how much creative tension you need to spur people to action. Every business and industry is different. But this is a choice that you should not leave to chance.

How are you motivating everyone in your business to think like winning competitors? In the remainder of this chapter, we will consider a menu of techniques to spur innovation. Read down this list and ask yourself if you're doing enough to bring out the best in your people by transforming them into winning competitors.

> ## How Are You Motivating Everyone to Think Like Winning Competitors?

Assigning Stretch Goals

The most common way of motivating competitive behavior is to set tough goals. In essence, you are asking people—much as you would an Olympic athlete—to compete against their past levels of personal performance. Some business leaders refer to challenge goals; others talk about big hairy audacious goals.[5] Regardless of the term, the concept is the same. Business as usual or incremental improvements is not enough. There's only one way to have a chance of meeting such aggressive targets: doing something completely different. Following Bob Johnstone's cornered-rat theory of creativity, you must innovate your way to success.

CEO John Seffrin embraced this concept when, in 1996, he challenged the American Cancer Society's eight thousand employees and 3 million volunteers with his 2015 goals: reduce cancer deaths by 50 percent, reduce incidence rates by 25 percent, and measurably improve the quality of life of cancer survivors. When the society was falling short of these goals, executives brainstormed to find innovations that could define a way forward. A completely new strategy was born: Access to Care. The result: more than 250,000 additional lives saved since the 2015 goals were announced. Without the creative tension generated by these stretch goals, this burst of innovation would never have occurred.

Stretch goals are especially important in larger companies. You must not allow people to hide in the comfort of bureaucracy. Employees at General Motors, once the largest and most profitable company in its industry, became "comfortable, insular, self-referential, and too wedded to the status quo."[6] Their inability to compete, which ultimately led the company to bankruptcy, was the manifestation of a mind-set that had become complacent. In contrast, Toyota executives pride themselves on setting goals that are nearly unattainable. They credit much of the company's growth and innovation over two decades to this practice.[7] But Toyota's quality problems—as executives pushed stretch goals for growth—remind us of the importance of setting strategic boundaries as essential countervailing safeguards (see the discussion of Toyota's violation of strategic boundaries in the previous chapter).

Ranking Individuals

A former student of mine works at a market-leading technology company in Silicon Valley. This business, which has grown rapidly to more than twenty-five thousand employees, is widely admired for its entrepreneurial vision and bold innovation.

Kathleen enjoys her new job and the people she works with. But she had one surprise when she joined this company fresh out of business school: an unexpected and unrelenting emphasis on performance reporting and ranking. Not only does the company carefully set and measure individual goals on a quarterly basis, but it requires department and business heads to "stack rank" the performance of all individuals who report to them. Rather than merely giving people a qualitative performance assessment ("meets minimum requirements," "surpasses expectations," and so on), managers rank their people from best to worst. A similar ranking across business units also rates the performance of people doing similar jobs in different groups.

These rankings affect who is promoted, who is placed on probationary performance-improvement plans, and who is asked to leave. "Management keeps pushing for more," Kathleen says, "and it's up to you to figure out what's next. You have to keep coming up with new ideas. It's a pressure cooker."

Many companies use similar approaches. But most people—including many managers—have not given much thought to why such techniques are so common in high-innovation firms.

Most of us rate our direct reports above average on performance evaluations. A high score avoids difficult conversations and keeps relationships cordial. It's easier to live in a world described in Garrison Keillor's radio series, *A Prairie Home Companion,* where, "all the women are strong, all the men are good looking, and all the children are above average."

In the real world, not everyone can be above average. And allowing subpar performance to go unchallenged can have insidious consequences. When James Kilts took over as CEO of Gillette in 2001, he discovered that more than two-thirds of Gillette executives had been rated in the highest possible category, earning maximum bonuses. Kilts was forced to reconcile these assessments with reality: Gillette had missed its earnings estimates for fifteen consecutive quarters.[8]

The forced ranking of subordinates makes difficult conversations unavoidable. More importantly, sharing the rankings motivates everyone to improve: by working harder, emulating those who are more successful, and experimenting to find better ways of doing their jobs.

Such discipline can be hard to accept. Toyota's newly hired American employees become visibly uncomfortable when they see the colored bar charts posted on the factory walls that show the relative performance of individual workers. But at Toyota, these charts serve an important role: new employees learn who they should watch as they learn the ropes, and, in keeping with Toyota's unique culture, more experienced employees help those who are falling behind.[9]

Jack Welch is widely credited with inventing this ranking system. GE ranked individuals semiannually and dismissed the bottom 5 percent if they didn't improve. Welch stated, "The ranking system was very controversial. Weed out the weakest. The Red Sox and Mets are playing tonight. Guess what? They're not putting on the field the guys in the minors. It's all about fielding the best team. It's been portrayed as a cruel system. It isn't. The cruel system is the one that doesn't tell anybody where they stand."[10]

You must be aware of the potential for abuse if rankings, like other techniques I discuss in this chapter, are used improperly. You want to generate creative tension, not destructive behavior. Forcing too many people into a low-performance category or mechanically linking scores to punishments can lead to trouble. Enron's CEO

Jeff Skilling took his "rank and yank" system to an extreme by identifying and firing the bottom 15 percent of employees every six months. Not surprisingly, employees were unwilling to challenge superiors about questionable deals or the accounting accruals that were being used to inflate short-term profits.[11]

Ranking Units

You can adapt the individual ranking approach by ranking teams and business units. In doing so, you will stir up adrenaline to search for best practices. Nike CEO Mark Parker claims that he likes to fire up friendly rivalries by posting each footwear division's performance scores after every season: "People see each other's scores, and they huddle and really look at how they can make it better next season."[12]

I first witnessed this technique in action while sitting in the office of Göran Lindahl, head of Swiss energy giant ABB's power-generation business (Lindahl was subsequently appointed ABB's CEO). We were discussing the methods he used to promote innovation and best-practices sharing among the managers of the twenty worldwide plants that reported to him.

He showed me a bar chart that he had recently sent out to the plant managers. The vertical axis reported "power transformer throughput time," and the horizontal axis showed the results of each plant.

Lindahl explained how he selected three different variables to measure each month and sent out comparative charts to all managers whose operations were being compared: "I don't even have to say anything. Those managers will fight like crazy to improve so they won't be low man on the ranking."[13]

Such innovation was also evident at the American Cancer Society where the thirteen regions were ranked on a variety of performance measures. When one division learned that another was generating much higher usage rates for its 1-800 patient-support numbers, the low-scoring division manager was immediately on the telephone with his counterpart to learn what that division was doing and how he could modify and improve his own system to leverage these ideas.[14]

SHARING INNOVATIONS ACROSS UNITS

At the same time you're ramping up internal competitive pressures, you may also want to spur innovation across units. This may be desirable, for example, if you want to boost revenues through cross-selling, share best practices to reduce expenses, or foster new product development across existing platforms and brands. Generating creative tension can spur such cross-unit innovation.

How Do You Encourage Innovation Across Units?

How do you encourage innovation across units in your business? Here are some techniques to consider. As you scan this list, ask yourself whether you're doing enough to build the level of creative tension needed to support your strategy.

Setting Span of Accountability Greater than Span of Control

One of the nostrums of management theory is that authority should equal responsibility. Put another way, the span of accountability (measures) should equal the span of control (resources). While this long-standing prescription seems reasonable, it is entirely the wrong formula for stimulating innovation across units.

Consider Siebel Systems, the originator of customer relationship management (CRM) software. The company designed and sold complex software, but relied on alliance partners for product installation and training. Individual managers at Siebel were responsible for only narrow slices of the business: product development, a specialized industry group, or corporate marketing. As one business unit head stated, "To do my day-to-day job, I depend on sales, sales consulting, competency groups, alliances, technical support, corporate marketing, field marketing, and integrated marketing communications.

None of these functions reports to me and most do not even report to my group. Coordination happens because we all have customer satisfaction as our first priority."[15]

No single manager at Siebel Systems controlled all the resources needed to satisfy a customer. Yet everyone was accountable for customer satisfaction, and all bonuses were keyed to this critical measure. In other words, the span of accountability (customer satisfaction) was much wider than the span of control (resources under a manager's direct control).

Does this make sense? Can it be fair to hold someone accountable for a measure they don't control?

There is method to this madness. To succeed in their jobs and ensure that customers were happy, managers at Siebel had no choice but to be creative in finding ways to get the resources they needed. They had to build personal relationships with others in the organization. They were forced to innovate to meet customer needs.

This example is not unique. Today more than ever, executives are holding subordinates accountable for broad measures such as customer satisfaction or brand revenue, even though individuals control only narrow subsets of resources. In an age of empowerment, when we want people to be entrepreneurial, this is exactly the right thing to do. In fact, my colleague Howard Stevenson defines entrepreneurship as "the process by which individuals—either on their own or inside organizations—pursue opportunities without regard to the resources they currently control."[16]

If you want your people to act as entrepreneurs—to work with others inside your organization to innovate—hold them accountable for measures they don't fully control.

Allocating Costs

Jamie Dimon, CEO of JPMorgan Chase, is widely credited with guiding his firm—225,000 people operating six worldwide businesses—through the treacherous waters of the 2008 to 2009 financial meltdown. Dimon uses a variety of techniques to ensure ongoing innovation. One technique that he insists on is full allocation of all corporate overhead costs. "Jamie wants all corporate costs, from legal to marketing, allocated to all the businesses in relation to how much they use them, to ensure that the businesses are truly profitable after all the overhead expenses," says Jay Mandelbaum, head of strategy and marketing.[17]

I originally learned the power of this technique from Percy Barnevik, former CEO of ABB. Barnevik, like Dimon, insisted that all corporate costs were allocated down the line to the divisions and profit centers that consumed services. Barnevik went one step further. He also allocated cost-of-capital charges to business profit centers and required division managers to calculate depreciation using replacement cost valuation, resulting in a higher depreciation charge and lower profits.

It wasn't obvious to me why these accounting allocations were so important until I began discussing the implications with division managers and business heads who were on the receiving end. What do you think happens when a business head, accountable for stretch profit targets, is forced to bear the burden of cost allocations that originate in other units? All of a sudden, managers on the receiving end care deeply about the spending decisions that the originating units are making.

Managers forced to absorb the costs of other units will invariably involve themselves in discussions about the value of services provided and potential alternatives, such as outsourcing or technology automation. They will use external benchmarks to compare costs. The outcome will often include rethinking how units can work together to do something better, faster, or cheaper. Without the pressure of cost allocations, no one would have considered these innovations.

Creating Cross-Unit Teams and Task Forces

Another way of forcing people to think outside the box is to assign them to a second box. Organization design, by its nature, creates boxes and comfort zones. This problem has existed as long as there have been organization charts. Twenty-five years ago, Harold Geneen, CEO of ITT (who was the Jack Welch of his generation), wrote of the danger that "each box on the organization chart will become an independent fiefdom, with each vice president thinking of his own terrain, his own people, his own duties and responsibilities, and no one thinking of the company as a whole. What tends to happen is that one man says, 'My job is to do this, and that's all I know.'"[18]

To counter this tendency, Dennis Bakke, founder of international energy company AES, has argued that people should spend 80 percent of their time on their primary jobs and allocate the other 20 percent to task forces and special projects.[19] Bakke is not alone. Managers at 3M, Google, and GE have used this technique to force people to cross boundaries and develop shared solutions to foster cross-selling, improve service delivery, and rationalize duplicate services.

Merck CEO Richard Clark also used this technique to encourage Merck's sixty thousand employees in sales, R&D, and regulatory affairs to work more closely together to speed drug development and commercialization. He asked groups of people from different functions to focus on major disease categories and interact with doctors, patients, and insurers. He stated, "This is the way work should get done in companies. It's not up and down. You need people to work together."[20]

There are two benefits of setting up such cross-unit teams and task forces. First, when people interact with others in different regions and business units, they are forced out of their day-to-day routines. As they listen and learn from new people, they may see business opportunities differently. New ideas will emerge. Second, not only will they be emissaries representing their home units in the cross-unit team meetings, they will also return home with different ideas and innovations they have learned from their new colleagues.

Using Matrix Accountability

At the extreme, you may choose a matrix design in which every manager has two bosses: one boss may be a region head, the other a product market head. Everyone must then balance conflicting priorities.

This option forces new thinking across units that would otherwise not interact. New ways of dealing with problems and opportunities often emerge. Carly Fiorina, former CEO of HP, adopted such a matrix to encourage teamwork among executives. She felt that business managers were worrying only about their own product lines and not enough about the overall good of the company.[21] Procter & Gamble, a company that had previously been organized by region, adopted a matrix organization in the 1990s to give equal decision-making power to newly formed global product groups. The benefits from this approach included cost savings from integrating purchasing, manufacturing, and distribution; a closer working relationship with large customers such as Walmart; enhanced global R&D; and faster speed to market.[22]

KEEP IT SIMPLE

The techniques described—cost allocations, task forces, and dual-reporting arrangements—can create complex systems and structures. So, if you decide to use these techniques, it's important to ensure that they do not burden your business with unnecessary bureaucracy.

Consider cross-unit teams. Forcing people to devote significant attention to activities outside their primary job is a double-edged sword. On the positive side, it forces individuals to think outside the box and can spark innovation. On the negative side, by bringing together multiple parties with differing agendas, you may sacrifice simplicity and speed in decision making.

This is the tension that John Chambers, CEO of Cisco, is now facing. In an attempt to foster creative tension by making "everyone uncomfortable," Chambers has formed a committee structure that requires the company's top 750 executives to spend 30 percent of their time on initiatives outside their primary job responsibilities. Over fifty committees review new business opportunities and approve cross-business initiatives. But there are consequences to this complexity: executives must spend considerable time in meetings away from customers and operations. There have also been reports that key decisions affecting customers have slowed down, sometimes to the benefit of competitors like HP that have been able to act more quickly.[23]

While committees and dual-reporting relationships can spur innovation by including a variety of viewpoints, having multiple decision makers can also get in the way. When P&G's global product leaders sought to launch a new product quickly, they still had to get the green light from all the affected regions whose profit targets would be affected. As a result, many within P&G believed that too many people in the new matrix had veto power that slowed decision making. To confirm these suspicions, market share and profitability began falling. In 2005, P&G abandoned the matrix in favor of global business units, but not before poor results forced the resignation of CEO Durk Jager.[24]

As a result of similar difficulties, most companies eventually dismantle matrix organizations. Mark Hurd, Carly Fiorina's replacement as CEO at HP, undid HP's matrix to increase the speed of decision making and enhance accountability.

Have committees and dual reporting made your organization too complex? Matrix organizations can work, but they require special design attributes and heightened leadership skills.[25]

Have Committees and Dual Reporting Made Your Organization Too Complex?

After reading this list of techniques, do you feel that you've done enough to spur innovation in your company? How much creative tension is generated in your business? Are people on edge? Or is everyone just a little too complacent and comfortable?

SPURRING INNOVATION

Pushing people out of their comfort zones isn't easy. To *spur innovation*, you must fight organizational inertia by using the uncomfortable techniques I've described in this chapter.

But you must be aware of these techniques' potential for damage. Creative tension can, if executed badly, foster anxiety, fear, and a temptation to cut corners. So, if you use the techniques in this chapter, you must do three things to ensure that the pressure you are applying is productive and healthy.

First, your business must have strong core values (see chapter 2). People should know their minimum level of responsibility and how to make tough trade-offs.

Second, you must set clear boundaries (see chapter 4). People can have no uncertainty about the behaviors and actions that are unacceptable—and the consequences— as they stretch themselves to meet demanding goals.

Finally, you must create an environment where people throughout the business are committed to helping each other succeed. If you ask individuals to think outside the box and innovate, you must ensure that everyone will be willing to pitch in to help make it work.

Creating such an environment is the topic for the next chapter.

SIX

HOW COMMITTED ARE YOUR
EMPLOYEES TO HELPING
EACH OTHER?

It was a cold, clear, December morning when the wheels of Southwest Airlines flight WN 9 touched down at Houston's Hobby airport. Captain Brittan had already called ahead to alert ground crews of the large amount of mail and freight they would need to unload.

As the gate crew scrambled into position, Captain Brittan aggressively applied the brakes, deployed the spoilers, and reversed engine thrust. In the race to the gate, it was important to slow the aircraft as quickly as possible to allow the tight turn to the first available ramp.

Once the airplane stopped at the gate and the wheel braces were secured, everything happened quickly. Door locks were released, the jet bridge swung into place, and the luggage handlers unloaded bags into the waiting carts. Passengers began deplaning. Before the cleaning crew had a chance to enter the aircraft, flight attendants hurried up the aisle tidying each seat.

Captain Brittan climbed into the front bin. He helped the baggage handler unload the mail and freight as new passengers began to board. Gate agents asked if they could help as the new flight crew went through their departure checklist.

Barely fifteen minutes after arriving, the fully loaded aircraft pushed back from the gate. As the captain taxied to the runway for takeoff, the flight attendant began the safety demonstration.[1]

Across town, in a gleaming fifty-story Houston office tower, Enron energy traders were busy at work. Enron had announced five new trading jobs. The competition for these positions was intense. A new trader could earn as much as an experienced airline pilot, with the potential for a substantial bonus.

Individual bonuses were determined by business unit profitability and the ranked contribution of each employee in that unit. Employees spent a lot of time jockeying to transfer to more profitable groups. After every bonus season, the parking lot filled up with shiny new Porsches and BMWs.

The culture at Enron was mercenary and selfish. "I remember one trader going crazy because his bonus was only $500,000," an employee reported. "He was cursing and screaming and throwing things at his desk. He thought that because he was so brilliant, they should be paying him a lot more."[2]

As long as you made money for Enron, you were left alone. But sabotage among traders was common. When people got up to go to the restroom, they had to remember to lock their computer screens. Otherwise, someone might steal their trade or change the position on their trade to make them look bad.[3] As an employee stated, "You never helped one another. Everyone was in it for themselves. People stabbed you in the back." Diana Peters, an Enron employee, described the atmosphere: "Bring them in young, bring them in smart, drain them, and drop them."[4]

These two businesses—Southwest Airlines and Enron—are different in a number of ways. But there is one difference that is not determined by the nature of their industries. It's determined by leadership. At Southwest Airlines, everyone—from top to bottom—is committed to helping each other succeed. At Enron, it was the opposite: self-interest prevailed.

No matter what the nature of your business, this is a choice you can't avoid. You must decide what type of commitment your business needs. Then you must exert your leadership skills to make it happen. This is the sixth implementation imperative: *building commitment*. Do this correctly, and you will unleash powerful forces. Get it wrong, and your entire strategy can crumble under you.

At which end of the spectrum does your business fall? The next question—How committed are your employees to helping each other?—asks you to address this imperative explicitly.

How Committed Are Your Employees to Helping Each Other?

Only you can decide what type of commitment is needed to support your strategy. In some businesses, executives choose self-interest as the overriding philosophy and tailor rewards accordingly. And sometimes this is exactly the right thing to do. If you run a boutique investment bank, for example, you may choose to pay multimillion-dollar bonuses to your star rainmakers based solely on their individual revenue contributions. Collaboration is not important in a company where "you eat what you kill."

More generally, if you want people to focus on specific tasks without being distracted or if you wish to motivate individuals to search for arbitrage trading opportunities, rewarding self-interest is the right approach to follow. On a trading desk—whether it's bonds or energy futures—or in the pits of a telemarketing call center, it's every man (or woman) for himself in the personal quest to make money.

But you must use this approach with care. If you choose self-interest as an organizing concept, you should ensure that your core values and strategic boundaries are strong enough to inoculate your business against abuses. You don't want to be another Enron. As I discussed in chapter 2, core values should stipulate, at a minimum, a do-no-harm level of responsibility. In addition, strategic boundaries should stipulate the kinds of behavior that will get you fired.

Most organizations are not built on self-interest. If you operate a business where relationships with customers are important, or if you have a complex production technology—to name just two situations—you need everyone to pitch in to help achieve shared goals. Southwest's industry-leading ten-minute gate change would be impossible without strong commitment from all employees—from the pilot to cargo handlers—to help each other get the job done.

To build high levels of commitment to help each other succeed, you must balance conflicting tensions. The techniques described in the previous chapter, such as stretch goals and individual and group rankings, are designed to motivate people to think and act like winning competitors. But these techniques represent only one side of the equation. You must also create an environment in which people are willing to help others when asked. You need people to compete against themselves and each other to achieve their personal best, but also to compete alongside each other as team members with shared goals.

Building such commitment to collaborate requires both leadership and an understanding of human nature. Ken Iverson, famed CEO of steelmaker Nucor, once stated, "Every manager should be something of a psychologist. We're supposed to know what makes people tick, what they want, and what they need. And much of what people want and need resides in the subconscious."[5]

Failing to pay attention to motivation can lead to the pathology of rewarding A while hoping for B.[6] Even though you may be counting on people's willingness to help each other, your reward system may be motivating effort that puts little value on building such relationships.

THEORIES OF MOTIVATION

The first step in building high levels of commitment—whether to self or to others—is to clarify your theory of motivation.

As an undergraduate at McGill, I was greatly influenced by *The Human Side of Enterprise*, a 1960 book written by MIT professor Douglas McGregor.[7] McGregor contrasted two theories of motivation—Theory X and Theory Y. Theory X describes a management approach that relies on top-down direction and control.

It assumes people dislike work and avoid it if possible. Extrinsic rewards and threat of punishment are necessary to motivate people to achieve organizational objectives. Theory Y, by contrast, hypothesizes that work can be a source of satisfaction. In Theory Y, the intrinsic rewards from such things as personal achievement and a feeling of self-worth can create commitment to an organization's objectives.

If you want to build an organization based on self-interest, Theory X is the approach to follow. Tie money to results, and people will respond to receive the promised rewards. This is the executive version of the stimulus-response experiments of psychologist B. F. Skinner who, in the 1930s, illustrated that rats can be trained to learn behaviors in anticipation of predictable rewards. Pay by formula for individual performance using commissions and bonuses, and withhold rewards from those who fail to deliver. As Enron's chairman Ken Lay stated, "An important part of our corporate culture is individualized compensation in each of our business units. There are big payouts."[8]

Money is always important. But you may have a more rounded view of human nature. You may believe that other things are important as well. In line with Theory Y, Mary Kay Cosmetics executives believe that their beauty consultants—2 million independent housewives and office workers—are motivated by five things reflected in the acronym STORM:

S: Satisfaction with a task well done (self-worth)

T: Teamwork (a sense of belonging)

O: Opportunity (to succeed)

R: Recognition

M: Money

Mary Kay executives work diligently to ensure that their company provides the tools to support all five STORM motivators: a constant flow of training and promotional sales aids (opportunity to succeed), events and conferences (self-worth), sales force activities and weekly meetings (teamwork), recognition and prizes (recognition), and financial incentives (money).

Money is certainly on the list, but it's not alone. As Mary Kay Ash, the founder of the company, noted when describing her personal theory of motivation, "A $5 ribbon plus $20 worth of recognition is worth more than a $25 prize."[9]

What Is Your Theory of Motivation?

What is your theory of motivation? What do you believe motivates people to work hard and contribute to the goals of your business? Every executive has a theory, but rarely discusses it or makes it explicit. Once your theory of motivation is clear in your own mind, the next step is to assess how good a job you've done applying it.

CREATING SHARED RESPONSIBILITY FOR SUCCESS

If your theory of motivation and your strategy both center on money and self-interest, your task is relatively easy. But what if your strategy requires people to help each other? Can you use money to motivate people to collaborate?

Cisco's CEO John Chambers describes how he did just this: "I forced people to work with others they didn't get along with, and I stretched people in a lot of ways. We based compensation on their collaborative abilities, as opposed to individual performance. The first year we did that two of my top leaders got zero bonus. You can bet they learned quickly how to collaborate."[10]

This approach is difficult to sustain over time. In the short term, people will respond to rewards and punishments. But this does not create commitment. It is pure stimulus–response. Without constant monitoring and the threat of withholding rewards, people will soon revert to old habits.

If you want to build commitment to helping others into the fabric of your organization, you must follow a different approach. Military leaders understand this well. They invest heavily in carefully designed practices based on the psychological principles that Ken Iverson referred to. There is good reason for their investment. Consider the U.S. Marine Corps. In battle conditions, when marines may be asked to take life-threatening risks, it is of paramount importance that every marine has confidence that those around him will come to his aid in times of distress. As the saying goes, soldiers don't die for their country; they die to help the friend beside them on the battlefield. Military leaders know that if you want to build an organization with high levels of commitment, it must have four attributes: pride in purpose, identification with the group, trust, and fairness.

Business leaders can adopt the same approach. Let's use two companies—Southwest Airlines and steelmaker Nucor—to illustrate these principles in action. Southwest is well known as today's most successful U.S. airline, rising from a Texas start-up to become the nation's most highly valued carrier with thirty-six years of consecutive profitability. It also boasts the most passengers flown and a market value that exceeds the other big six U.S. carriers combined.

Nucor is a minimill that, like Southwest, revolutionized its industry and now dominates it. You may be skeptical about using a rust-belt steel company as a best-practices example. But before rushing to judgment, consider what *BusinessWeek* reported in 2006:

> Nucor has nurtured one of the most dynamic and engaged workforces around. The 11,300 nonunion employees don't see themselves as worker bees waiting for instructions from above. Nucor's flattened hierarchy and emphasis on pushing power to the front line lead its employees to adopt the mindset of owner-operators. It's a profitable formula: Nucor's 387% return to shareholders over the past five years handily beats almost all other companies in the Standard & Poor's 500-stock index, including New Economy icons Amazon.com, Starbucks, and eBay. And the company has become more profitable as it has grown. Margins, which were 7% in 2000, reached 10% last year.[11]

Let's consider what the leaders in these organizations have done to build consistently high levels of commitment to help others succeed. As you read this list, ask yourself to what extent you have (or should have) applied these techniques in your business.

Pride in Purpose

If people are proud of their organization's mission and the broader purpose it represents, they will want to assume shared responsibility for its success. This includes helping others succeed in doing their jobs well.

The Marine Corps, like many elite fighting units, puts enormous emphasis on its mission and history as a means of creating pride in purpose. Every marine stands proud to the words "Semper Fidelis" [Always Faithful] and "First to Fight" that declare the resolve of the corps' storied past.

Businesses can also leverage such pride in purpose. Southwest Airlines employees are visibly proud of their origins as a David and Goliath upstart out to beat the major airlines. Their motto: "We're giving America the freedom to fly." Similarly, minimill Nucor came out of nowhere to overtake large, integrated competitors such as Bethlehem Steel. Nucor's Iverson talks about the pride that comes from being part of a successful enterprise: "We share a higher cause."

Many companies use simple slogans to signal their pride. Merck's mission of "putting patients first" or Amazon's desire to "create the most customer-centric business on earth" are designed to instill pride among employees. So does the mission of the American Cancer Society to eliminate cancer, save lives, and diminish suffering. As an ACS executive stated, "We've been able to demonstrate that we're making a difference, and that provides the ultimate motivation."[12]

Identification with the Group

Belonging to an elite organization is a badge of distinction that carries with it the responsibility to help others in the group. The first loyalty of every marine is to his unit—to help his fellows under any and all circumstances—followed by loyalty to the corps, God, and country. A marine is a member of an elite organization and is constantly reminded of this fact. As the Marine Corps slogan says, "The Few. The Proud."

The elite Army Rangers similarly proclaim, "Never shall I fail my comrades." The desire to belong to such a group can be a powerful motivator. And the desire to help your team or unit is a powerful and uncompromising force.

Businesses can apply the same principle of exclusivity. Southwest Airlines offers jobs to less than 2 percent of the hundred thousand people who apply annually, leading one observer to claim that it's more difficult to be accepted at Southwest Airlines than at Harvard.[13] Southwest employees take pride in the difficult selection process that must be passed to be admitted to their elite group.

Executives at Southwest reinforce this high level of identification with the company by routinely asking employees to participate in hiring decisions. Employees from various departments interview job candidates and can veto any applicants whom they feel would not be a good fit.

At Nucor, employees also consider themselves part of an exclusive group. When Nucor placed an ad in the local newspaper seeking job applications for its mill in

South Carolina, the line blocked the road into the plant. When the plant manager couldn't make his way to work, he called the police to request help with the traffic jam. He was told that police were short-staffed because three of their own officers were in the line applying for Nucor jobs.[14]

Trust

When you trust someone, you're willing to make yourself vulnerable: to share personal or confidential information and put your reputation on the line to support him. If you trust someone, you are confident that your actions won't come back to haunt you. The flip side, of course, is that if you don't trust someone, you will not be willing to help him.

For a marine, the ultimate trust is knowing that someone is watching your back as you move into danger. You are making yourself vulnerable with full confidence that your fellow marines will protect you—with their lives if necessary.

Businesses cannot ask as much of employees as the Marine Corps can. But the same principle can apply. Executives can earn the trust of their employees by their day-to-day actions. At Nucor, executives encourage employees to propose innovations to improve efficiency. Many companies would use any resulting efficiency gains to reset production targets and then require workers to produce more for the same pay. In contrast, Nucor does not use efficiency improvements that employees suggest to lower production-based pay scales. Instead, it shares the financial savings from such innovations with employees, with no upper limit. Over time, this policy has built trust among workers that employees and executives are truly working together toward the same shared goals. As a result, union organizers find a chilly reception when they stand outside Nucor facilities trying to recruit workers.

Fairness

The final requirement for collaboration is fairness. If you go out of your way to help someone in your business, and he or she receives all the rewards and you receive nothing, are you likely to be willing to help him or her again? The answer, I suspect, would be no.

Disparity in pay policies is the most obvious challenge to fairness. If there are notable winners and losers when payday comes, people will not collaborate. For this reason, the pay scale in the marines is flat—everyone knows what others are making and it's pretty much the same.

But pay is easy to fix. More insidious are the perks that signal that those "on top" are more deserving than people lower in the hierarchy.

Nucor's Iverson described the dangers of: "Ivory tower office suites. Executive parking spaces. Employment contracts. Corporate jets. Limousines. First-class travel. Meetings at posh resorts. Company cars. Executive dining rooms. The people at the top of the corporate hierarchy grant themselves privilege after privilege, flaunt those privileges before the men and women who do the *real* work, then wonder why employees are unmoved by management's invocations to cut costs and boost profitability."[15]

To guard against this danger, Southwest's top executives work out of small interior offices adjacent to their Dallas airport. One industry observer described their accommodations as only marginally nicer than a janitor's closet.[16] For the same reason, Tom Watson Sr., the legendary CEO who built IBM to greatness in his thirty-year tenure, made all managers and executives remove their titles and ranks from their office doors and desks and eliminated executive parking spaces.

How good a job have you done in building commitment among your employees to help each other? As a leader, there's a lot you must get right. You must communicate a pride in purpose about the work you do together, you must build a sense among your employees that they belong to an exclusive group, you must be trustworthy and expect the same from others, and you must create an ethic of fairness when it's time to share rewards. As they say in the Marine Corps, officers eat last.

Which of these principles are you applying? How are you creating shared responsibility for success? What's standing in the way of high levels of commitment to help others in your business?

> **How Are You Creating Shared Responsibility for Success?**

COMPENSATION AND COMMITMENT

Using compensation to motivate self-interest is straightforward. Pay people for results. But the interaction between compensation and commitment to helping others is more complicated. There are two issues you must consider: rewarding team performance and disparity between top earners and others.

Rewarding Team Performance

Rewarding team results can be a simple and effective way of motivating people to help others. Southwest pays pilots and flight crews by the trip rather than by the hour. This encourages everyone to work together to turn around the plane quickly at the gate.[17] Everyone understands that he or she wins as a team.

At Nucor, employees receive bonuses based on daily team production. Salaries in the mills are set below the industry average, but there is no upside limit to bonuses, which often triple base pay. Production numbers are posted daily and followed closely.

As Iverson described, "Work groups set their own goals for exceeding the baseline and work out their own ways of pursuing them, guided only by this certainty: The more they produce, the more they earn. They have a simple stake in the business. Like most successful entrepreneurs, our employees are enthusiastic, energetic, and dead earnest about their work."[18]

The pressure to perform—and do the job right—is intense, but it comes from the group, not from management. In fact, at Nucor, it's impossible for an observer to tell who the team supervisor is. Since supervisors share the same bonuses as workers, they pitch in with everyone else to help meet and surpass team goals.

Higher up the ladder, Nucor managers and executives apply the same principles to their own compensation: they share in gains in good years and losses in downturns. At every level, base salaries are lower—but bonus potential is higher—than industry averages. Division managers receive bonuses based on their division's return on assets; executives receive bonuses based on company return on shareholders' equity.

Stock ownership—through vesting or stock options—can also be an effective tool to motivate a focus on shared goals. At Southwest Airlines, employees at all levels receive stock options, which they are allowed to sell whenever they like. As former CEO Jim Parker stated, "If you can't sell it, you don't really own it."[19]

This freedom-to-sell philosophy goes against the practices followed at companies such as AIG and Citigroup. AIG's Hank Greenberg awarded generous stock grants to top employees but required them to keep the shares.[20] Similarly, Sandy Weill rewarded Citigroup managers with stock, but forbade them from selling. Chuck Prince, the CEO who followed Weill, described his predecessor's compensation philosophy, "The flag was nailed to the mast; if the ship went down, you went down with it."[21]

Disparity Between Top Earners and Others

Nothing will kill someone's desire to help others faster than resentment due to inequities in pay. If people in your business believe that pay is unjustly rewarding some at the expense of others, their resentment is inevitable. And when there's resentment, people will be unwilling to collaborate. (Recall the unflattering picture of the Enron trader described at the beginning of this chapter.)

The DaimlerChrysler merger failed in large part because of resentment caused by pay practices. The merger was intended to allow managers in the two companies to share knowledge and build synergies across product platforms. But in 1997, the year before the merger, Chrysler CEO Bob Eaton earned $16 million, while Daimler-Benz CEO Jürgen Schrempp earned $2 million. To rub salt in the wound, Eaton pocketed an additional $70 million for effecting the merger, while Schrempp got nothing.[22] Similar disparities existed between American and German managers at all levels of the company. Resentment from the inequities in compensation killed any interest in working collaboratively.

Such horizontal pay inequity—disparity between people doing similar jobs—is corrosive to collaboration. A "winner-take-all" approach—where top performers get the lion's share of the rewards—is fine if you are building an organization based on self-interest. This is the right thing to do in certain circumstances. We don't expect Roger Federer to help lower-seeded tennis players improve their game. But this approach will inevitably destroy any attempt to create shared responsibility for success.

The second threat to fairness is vertical pay inequity. If you are a highly paid executive, there's a good chance that your compensation is part of the problem. During the 1990s, corporate profits rose by 114 percent, while average CEO pay rose by 570 percent and worker pay rose by 37 percent.[23] By 2008, CEO pay averaged more than 340 times that of frontline workers, up from 25 times in 1981.[24] What kind of signal are you sending if the pay of your CEO and top executives is vastly out of proportion to the compensation everyone else in your organization receives?

If you want people to commit to helping each other, you must share rewards fairly. Southwest executives operate with a rule that they will receive pay increases that are proportionately no larger than the amounts other employees receive. In bad times, executives take pay reductions like everyone else.[25] As a result of this policy, Southwest executives generate ten times more revenue per dollar of executive compensation than do their counterparts at the other big U.S. carriers.[26]

Your pay—and its relationship to employees lower in your business—will be put under a microscope in hard times. Nucor's CEO bragged about being the lowest-paid *Fortune* 500 CEO during an industry downturn. While Nucor department heads had taken pay cuts up to 40 percent and company officers were down 50 percent to 60 percent, Iverson cut his own pay by 75 percent. Iverson stated, "We not only *shared* the pain, we doled out the lion's share to the people at the top."[27]

If you want people to embrace your vision of shared success, you must be perceived as a leader who values fairness and equity above self-interest. For this reason, Sam Palmisano, when taking over as CEO of IBM, asked the board to reallocate half his bonus to other executives who would be leaders of his new, team-based strategy. Palmisano announced in the spring of 2009, when the country was still reeling from recession, that 250,000 IBM employees would be getting raises. But, he added, "The executives won't—but that's fine. We make enough money!"[28]

How Do Your Compensation Policies Affect Commitment to Help Others?

How do your compensation policies affect commitment to help others? Do pay inequities create resentments that block people's willingness to help each other?

BUILDING COMMITMENT

The questions in this chapter may be difficult for you to accept. They ask a lot of you. You must understand human psychology, articulate your personal theory of motivation, and exercise the leadership skills of a marine commander.

But if you want to satisfy the sixth implementation imperative—*building commitment*—half-measures won't do. If you can answer the questions in this chapter to your own satisfaction, you're on your way to creating an organization that is both mission focused and resilient.

The stage is now set for the final imperative and the topic of the final chapter—adapting to change.

SEVEN

WHAT STRATEGIC UNCERTAINTIES KEEP YOU AWAKE AT NIGHT?

Only three things in life are certain: (1) death, (2) taxes, and (3) the fact that today's strategy won't work tomorrow. At some point in the future, your products will become obsolete, your customers' tastes will change, technology will render your business model uncompetitive. Today's successes will be tomorrow's old news. The question is not if, but when.

The changing composition of the Dow Jones Industrial Average is a reminder of the fleeting fortunes of business. If you look back twenty-five years, you will find that fewer than half the companies on that list are still prominent today. Companies such as Bethlehem

Steel, Eastman Kodak, Sears Roebuck, and Woolworth have fallen by the wayside.

Few companies seem capable of adapting to change. Most cling to ways that were successful in the past until they're pushed over the edge into oblivion. What about your business? Can you anticipate change and reinvent yourself to stay competitive? Or will your company be a footnote in the history of successful businesses?

In this final chapter, we will consider the techniques of companies that have adapted and prospered over decades. One such company is Johnson & Johnson. In chapter 2, I discussed J&J's credo, which concludes with the sentence, "When we operate according to these principles, the stockholders should realize a fair return."

How have Johnson & Johnson stockholders fared? If you had purchased a single share of J&J stock in 1944, the year the company went public, you would have paid $37.50. That was quite a lot of money when a postage stamp cost three cents and Coke was a nickel. In fact, the price of your J&J share would be the equivalent of about $450 today—roughly the price of a Google share.

But you would not regret your purchase. With stock splits, your single share would have multiplied to become twenty-five hundred shares today. If you had reinvested your dividends, your holding would now be worth more than $900,000.[1]

We could marvel at the annualized return over sixty-five years (in excess of 17 percent), but the real story is this company's ability to adapt in an industry that has seen technological upheaval, intense government regulation, and fierce international competition. This is not a market for the faint of heart.

How has Johnson & Johnson managed to prevail when so many others have ended up in the corporate graveyard? The answer is simple. Executives at Johnson & Johnson know how to ask the right questions . . . and then act.

Adapting to change is the final implementation imperative. To adapt successfully over the long term, you must learn how to ask the right questions to ensure that people in your business are constantly anticipating—and responding—to the changes that surround you. This leads to the final question—What strategic uncertainties keep you awake at night?

Worry is part of the job description of every executive. Executives at Johnson & Johnson even worry that people in their company don't worry enough. As former CEO

What Strategic Uncertainties Keep You Awake at Night?

Ralph Larsen commented, "Everybody at the company had read these wonderful stories about us, how we were one of the ten most admired companies. The company got very good press, much of which was deserved, some of which was not. But it led, I felt, to an unhealthy sense of well-being in the company. It's very tough to get people to change when they think everything is wonderful."[2]

Your job is to stimulate change by making worry both healthy and productive. You want people to worry—but their worry should focus on things that could upset your current strategy. To adapt successfully, you must activate an ongoing focus on strategic uncertainties—the threats and contingencies that could invalidate the assumptions underpinning your strategy. Then, and only then, will people be prepared to act decisively—and adapt—when necessary.

Failure to pay attention to strategic uncertainties has caused the demise of more than one of Johnson & Johnson's competitors. In one company, a medical device business, executives focused their attention on a bonus scheme that would pay rich rewards if the company achieved key sales and earnings targets. They became so focused on shipments of existing products that they failed to watch technology developments. While they were managing the business to hit their short-term numbers, J&J managers were investigating the implications of a new technology that was emerging in an adjacent industry. Before the medical device executives knew what hit them, J&J had overtaken them in the market. The hapless competitor was left with obsolete products and no clear path forward.[3]

Examples of this type of failure—failure to focus your entire organization on the strategic uncertainties that surround you—are all too plentiful. Consider AOL. As the company struggled to evolve beyond a provider of dial-up services, executives took comfort in the belief that any move to broadband would be a slow erosion. Without the urgent prodding of executives, people in the business failed to address the strategic uncertainties that would eventually lead to their undoing. Not only did Google and Yahoo win the bulk of online advertising dollars, new competitors such as Facebook and YouTube fundamentally changed the role of online access and communication services.[4] AOL, which had started with a commanding competitive lead, is now far behind in the race.

The failure to gather and respond to strategic uncertainties was also at the root of the 2008 to 2009 financial crisis. Signals of an asset bubble existed, but they either were not picked up or were ignored. Very few firms—Goldman Sachs and JPMorgan Chase were the notable exceptions—were able to focus the attention of their organizations on these threats.

Strategic uncertainties—changes that could invalidate your strategy—are different for every industry and every business. At Microsoft, executives worry about the impact of the Internet on their stand-alone software products. Executives at Google worry about government regulation amid accusations of monopoly abuse. In the newspaper industry, changes in delivery technology and the underlying health of advertisers keep executives awake at night. In retail, it's changes in channels and consumer purchasing patterns.

SIGNALING YOUR PRIORITIES

If you're like most executives, you can easily identify the strategic uncertainties that could threaten your current strategy. The challenge is how to get the message across to everyone in your business. You need to motivate what Larry Bossidy calls "the relentless quest for the critical one percent of information that can make all the difference to your business prospects."[5]

How Do You Focus Everyone's Attention on These Uncertainties?

How do you focus everyone's attention on these uncertainties? Focusing attention relies on a simple truth: everyone watches what the boss watches. As the saying goes, "What interests my boss fascinates me!"

Everything you do sends a signal. People are always watching you for cues as to what you think is important, for guidance about where they should spend their time. So, if you want people to focus on a specific set of issues, focus on those issues yourself. Visibly and consistently. This will signal to everyone how important these issues are to you and your company.

This simple approach became clear to me when I interviewed the CEO of a major pharmaceutical company. He was explaining his company's strategy and the uncertainties that kept him awake at night: global expansion, the ability to integrate a large acquisition, and difficulties the company was facing in integrating technology.

As we were talking, he picked up a brown leather binder from his desk and showed me tabs for key issues and accountabilities he monitored personally. He explained how the things he monitored mapped into his weekly meeting agenda and the questions and issues he raised with subordinates.

When I returned six weeks later to interview managers one and two levels down who reported to the CEO, what do you think I discovered? Everyone had a brown leather binder. The CEO had not handed out these binders. Instead, everyone had figured out that the only way to satisfy the boss was to replicate his personal information system.

This simple phenomenon—paying attention to what your boss watches—has important strategic implications. When people went into regularly scheduled operating meetings with the CEO and he opened his brown leather binder, everyone was prepared.

Because they knew what strategic uncertainties he was monitoring, they could anticipate his questions and, in the interactive discussion that followed, offer interpretations for new trends—both positive and negative—as well as action plans. Occasionally, these ideas formed the seeds for a new strategic initiative.

What is your brown leather binder? What tools are you using to signal where you want people to search for disruptive change? If you focus consistently on the same set of data—asking questions and probing—so will everyone else in your business. This should rank as one of the most important things you do.

INTERACTIVE CONTROL SYSTEMS

Every organization has a variety of performance measurement systems: profit plans, balanced scorecards, human resource systems, cost accounting systems, and so on. Most of these can, and should, be used diagnostically. You can safely delegate the operation of these systems to staff specialists and limit your involvement to setting annual goals and reviewing periodic exception reports.

Interactive control systems are different. They are the information systems—like the brown leather binder—you watch consistently and visibly. Because they're so important to you, they become a primary focus of attention for everyone in your business.

You can use any information system interactively. It could be a brown leather binder, a profit plan, or a new-business booking system. Your choice. But the system must have four characteristics to be effective in controlling interactively: it must (1) contain simple and easy-to-understand information, (2) require face-to-face interaction between operating managers, (3) focus debate and dialogue on strategic uncertainties, and (4) generate new action plans.

At Johnson & Johnson, executives have chosen to use their profit-planning systems interactively. Four times each year, managers at each of J&J's operating companies estimate and reestimate their profit plans and second-year forecasts. Working systematically from the bottom of the organization to the top, everyone is challenged to rework numbers as circumstances change and defend his or her revised estimates.

As part of the process, managers also develop and defend new five- and ten-year forecasts that focus on only four numbers: unit sales volume, sales revenue, net income, and return on investment. They revisit these numbers again and again for the same two years (for example, 2015 and 2020) during subsequent annual planning processes.

How does this interactive process work? Imagine the conversation that occurs when a J&J sector executive visits an operating company to review the revised five- and ten-year plan. "Let me understand this, Roy. Last year, you told me that your best estimate for 2015 revenue was $425 million. Today, you're revising that estimate down to $350 million."

The next question is predictable: "What has changed?" The answer, of course, depends on the nature of the business and its changing circumstances. Was the downward revision due to the entry of a new competitor? Changes in a licensing agreement? Or, changes in health care legislation that could affect margins? Conversely, the surprise might be in the other direction. Instead of forecasting a shortfall in revenue, managers might be predicting an unexpected increase. Was the unexpected good news due to the discovery of a new technology? The exit of a competitor? Or increase in demand for a newly discovered use?

The first question is, "What has changed?" The second question is, "Why?" The third—and most critical—question is, "What are you going to do about it?"

This is where the interactive process begins to pay dividends. Because managers knew what questions to expect—Johnson & Johnson has applied the same questioning process consistently over many years—they had already developed tentative action plans. They now focused the debate and dialogue on how to best deploy resources to deal with emerging opportunities and threats. Some responses were modest—incremental adjustments to strategies and plans. Others were significant, requiring capital investment or a fundamental reorientation in business direction.

Understanding the power of such interactive debate is not new. Over twenty-five years ago, ITT's Harold Geneen described the interactive meetings he chaired, "Not only did we learn and get help from one another, not only did we achieve speed and directness in handling our problems, but our meetings often were charged with such dynamism and enthusiasm that at times we worked with a feeling of sheer exhilaration. Generating new ideas that were not on anyone's agenda, we came up with new products, new ventures, new ways of doing things."[6]

Goldman Sachs follows just this approach. Its interactive control system—with its focus on strategic uncertainties—allowed Goldman to avoid the mortgage-backed securities debacle that brought most of its competitors to their knees. A Goldman executive described how it uses its profit and loss system interactively: "We look at the P&L of our business every day. We have lots of models that are important, but none are more important than the P&L, and we check every day to make sure our P&L is consistent with where our risk models say it should be. In December, our mortgage business lost money for 10 days in a row. It wasn't a lot of money, but by the tenth day we thought that we should sit down and talk about it."[7]

As the top fifteen Goldman executives pored over every trading position the firm held—debating back and forth to gain understanding—they began to feel that the problem would continue to worsen. The first two questions were the same ones asked at Johnson & Johnson. What has changed? Why? The answer was unsettling: the old strategy was no longer working.

Now, they asked the critical third question: "What are you going to do about it?" Going against the momentum in their industry, Goldman executives acted. They decided to reduce exposure to mortgage-backed securities and hedge remaining positions against future losses. This early action—based on the interactive use of a simple P&L—allowed the firm to adjust its strategy and prosper as competitors were forced into liquidation or to beg for long-term government bailouts.[8]

The Goldman Sachs example is also a reminder (and a caution) that success in one imperative does not lessen the need to attend to the other imperatives discussed in previous chapters. They are all interrelated. Goldman executives were skillful in using their interactive control system to steer their business away from the damage inflicted by the financial crisis. But they were later dogged by accusations of misleading investors following their decision to create and sell investment products that would profit if the housing market—and related mortgage-backed securities—declined.

An erosion of core values and lack of strategic boundaries were at the root of the problem. Through most of its history, Goldman had been organized as a partnership with the famously strong core value, "Our clients' interests always come first." In 1999, Goldman became a publicly traded company. With its new focus on shareholder value, many have questioned whether profit now takes precedence over client interests. Goldman had also, in the past, set clear strategic boundaries that forbade employees from engaging in transactions that could create conflicts of interest with clients. Current executives, rising from the ranks of the trading floor instead of traditional advisory services and investment banking, had abandoned these boundaries.[9]

CHOOSING WHICH SYSTEM
TO USE INTERACTIVELY

The strategic uncertainties that underpin your business strategy will determine which system you should use interactively. At Johnson & Johnson, it's a profit-planning system. At Goldman Sachs, a daily P&L. Every company is different—because every strategy is different. Sam Walton required regional managers to fly into Walmart's headquarters in Bentonville each week for face-to-face meetings to discuss newly released information on what was selling and not selling in Walmart stores and how its prices compared with competitors'. The interactive discussions that followed focused on threats and contingencies in local markets and action plans to respond.[10]

Executives of companies such as PepsiCo and Coca-Cola that create barriers to entry through brand marketing worry about how to extend the attractiveness of their mature products (remember New Coke?). These executives use their brand revenue systems interactively. They receive weekly updates of product shipments by region and pore over new data to learn what competitors are doing. In follow-up meetings, they focus on how to respond with changes in pricing, promotions, and packaging—often leading to new strategic initiatives.

Firms following different strategies face different strategic uncertainties. For example, companies following low-cost strategies often worry that new technologies could undermine their strategy. Executives at such firms use project management systems interactively to monitor competitors' product teardowns, learn about technological developments in other industries, and formulate proactive responses.

Pharmaceutical executives worry about changes in the rules of competition that could threaten patent-protected niches and high-margin products. These executives use in-house intelligence systems to gather information on changes in social, political, and technological environments that could have an impact on their current strategy.

Their interactive discussions focus on understanding emerging trends and developing action plans for product pricing and influencing new legislation.[11]

What system do you use interactively to stimulate change? If you can't answer this question, you are missing the most important catalyst for adapting to the disruptions that will—sooner or later—challenge your business strategy.

> What System Do You Use Interactively to Stimulate Change?

KEEP IT SIMPLE

The five- and ten-year plans at J&J focus on only four numbers, for good reason. To make the interactive process work, you must keep it simple. You cannot allow staff groups with complex scorecards and elaborate planning documents to hijack the process. If you allow such complexity to overwhelm the process, people will be prevented from focusing on the underlying issues. Instead of searching for changes in competitive trends, they will waste precious time trying to reconcile different calculations, understand assumptions, and determine the reliability of the data.

Jack Welch threw out the elaborate five-year planning documents staff groups had prepared in favor of simple statements of business challenges and proposed action plans that operating managers had put together.[12] At ADP, executives hone in on new initiatives with a series of "one-pagers"—discussion documents that focus on strategic uncertainties and action plans. The one-pagers circulate back and forth between the CEO and business heads to clarify thinking and action plans.[13]

TOP-DOWN QUESTIONING: BOTTOM-UP LEARNING

An interactive control system uses questioning from the top to stimulate the flow of information from the bottom—information that can help you and others learn about trends that could have an impact on the long-term health of your business. People close to technology, markets, and customers are the first to know about such changes. They can and must pass this information up the line for it to act as a catalyst for change.

For this process to work, you must ask people throughout your business to propose new ideas and action plans in response to changing circumstances. You must encourage everyone to share new information—some good, some bad—with his or her boss. This is not easy for two reasons.

First, people are busy. They won't naturally stop what they're doing to search for new information—and pass it up the line—unless their bosses demand that they engage in the interactive process. As a sector executive at Johnson & Johnson stated, "You have to force busy people to do this. Otherwise, they will be caught up in day-to-day activities—account visits, riding with salesmen, standing on the manufacturing floor."

Second, people may be nervous about sharing new ideas or voicing unpopular opinions. Lower-level managers may be reluctant to be the bearers of bad news. Others may be afraid to express opinions that challenge the boss's position. Some managers may fear losing their bonus if the company uses the new information to reset performance benchmarks.

Fear of competition—and worry about strategic uncertainties—is both healthy and necessary. But being afraid to voice your opinions and contribute your best ideas can mean only one thing: senior executives don't want to hear disconfirming views. Such blinders are a recipe for disaster.

As Goldman Sachs executives were making tough decisions to exit high-risk positions, Lehman Brothers CEO Richard Fuld continued to push to make Lehman the industry's top mortgage-securitization firm. People inside the business were getting nervous. A senior trader on the securitized mortgage desk recalled that, in early 2007, financial models began to show greatly increased delinquencies and defaults causing him and his colleagues to begin raising questions and concerns. But pressure from the top to keep driving growth made bad news something that executives didn't want to hear. As the trader recounted, "Anyone at our level who had a different view from senior management would find themselves going somewhere else quick. You are not paid to rock the boat."[14]

Intel's former CEO, Andy Grove, was insistent on confronting the fact that people will be reluctant to share bad news if they're afraid of their boss's reaction:

> Keep in mind that the key role of Cassandras is to call your attention to strategic inflection points, so under no circumstances should you ever "shoot the messenger," nor should you allow any manager who works for you to do so. I can't stress this issue strongly enough. It takes many years of consistent conduct to eliminate fear of punishment as an inhibitor of strategic discussion. It takes only one incident to introduce it. News of this incident will spread through the organization like wildfire and shut everyone up. Once the environment of fear takes over, it will lead to paralysis throughout the organization and cut off the flow of bad news from the periphery.[15]

Goldman Sachs was not the only financial services firm to adapt successfully during the 2008 to 2009 financial crisis. Jamie Dimon, CEO of JPMorgan Chase, is also credited with having the foresight to steer his firm clear of the worst of the financial crisis by exiting the subprime mortgage business early. Dimon's voracious efforts to understand strategic uncertainties is legendary. Bill Daley, head of corporate responsibility and former U.S. secretary of commerce recounted, "At my first operating committee meeting, I was shocked. People were challenging Jamie, debating him, telling him he was wrong. It was like nothing I'd seen in a Bill Clinton cabinet meeting, or anything I'd ever seen in business."[16]

For the interactive process to work, you must reward those individuals who have the courage to tell you bad news or suggest that your assumptions may be flawed. When new CEO Alan Mulally arrived at Ford, executives were afraid of admitting failure. Their presentations at Thursday morning meetings showcased only successes (color-coded green) and avoided problems (color-coded yellow and red). Mulally challenged his executives, asking how everything could be so successful when the company was losing billions. North America head Mark Fields then made a presentation noting technical problems with the new Ford Edge. Production delays would be inevitable. People in the room held their breath to see how their new boss would react. "The whole place was deathly silent." Mulally recalled, "Then I applauded and said, 'Mark, I really appreciate that clear visibility.' The next week, the entire set of charts was all rainbows."[17]

To get the information and insight you seek, you must encourage the people around you to challenge deeply held assumptions—even yours. This is often difficult because many of these assumptions seem closed to discussion. But at the root of every failed company is a set of assumptions that proved false. We assumed that housing prices never fall simultaneously across the country. We assumed asset diversification eliminates risk. We assumed the migration to digital media would be slow and orderly. We assumed customers wouldn't be willing to trade fewer features for lower price.

To encourage people to challenge assumptions and propose new ideas, Johnson & Johnson rewards people subjectively for participating in the interactive process. Former CEO Ralph Larsen explained, "We do not have a formula-driven compensation program, which probably makes us different than most companies. We pay people based on their long-term contribution to the business. It's highly subjective . . . a lot of judgment goes into it. We have people around here who are highly motivated, who will break their backs to do a great job, and who generally set tougher goals for themselves than we would ever set for them. To me it's demeaning and wrong to set tightly crafted financial objectives . . . Besides, it turns into a game, where people then want to keep the goal lower rather than higher."[18]

Rewarding subjectively—instead of using a pay-for-performance formula—brings four benefits that are essential for the interactive process. First, executives can reward people for the courage to voice unpopular opinions and propose novel solutions. Many of these ideas may not deliver measurable results in the short term. Second, subjective rewards encourage people to share their ideas and experiments with their bosses so that they can be recognized for their efforts. Third, assigning rewards subjectively demands that senior executives understand the competitive environment, the context for decisions, and alternatives that were not chosen. You cannot assign rewards fairly unless you have made a significant personal investment in learning about the business. Finally, subjective rewards help protect against the sandbagging and gaming that is inevitable when rewards are mechanically linked to performance.

Trust is also essential. Recall the discussion in the previous chapter. People will only commit to help each other—in this case, by sharing information—if they trust you. At Johnson & Johnson, executives push hard for new ideas in discussions, but there are safety valves built into their system. The credo, which outlines responsibilities to key constituents, provides a long-term perspective for all decisions. In addition, J&J builds a separate contingency line into each profit plan to buffer aggressive targets. If needed, managers can draw down the contingency rather than take risks that could imperil the business.

The president of one of Johnson & Johnson's operating companies summed up his perspective on its interactive profit planning system this way: "These meetings are very important. We should always be thinking about such issues, but it is tough when you are constantly fighting fires. The Johnson & Johnson system forces us to stop and really look at where we have been and where we are going. We know where the problems are. We face them every day. But these meetings force us to think about how we should respond and to look at both the upside and downside of changes in the business. They really get our creative juices flowing."[19]

How Do You Encourage Bottom-up Information Sharing?	How do you encourage bottom-up information sharing? Is everyone in your business moving information from the bottom of your organization to the top so that

you, and everyone around you, can be ready to anticipate change and adapt when necessary?

ADAPTING TO CHANGE

The final implementation imperative—adapting to change—is the most important. Nothing in your business is set in stone. Change is inevitable. The only question is whether you will be prepared. The interactive process allows you to focus your entire organization on the strategic uncertainties that will one day—sooner or later—invalidate your current strategy.

The debate, dialogue, and learning that surround this process will give you confidence to address—and change when necessary—the other six imperatives. The need to anticipate—and act—is the reason that I presented the ideas of this book as a series of questions to be debated and explored as the world around you evolves and changes.

You now know the seven questions and the reasons why each is important. To execute your strategy successfully, you must cut through the complexity that clouds clear thinking. Simplify. Make tough choices. Choose a primary customer. Prioritize your core values. Select a handful of truly critical performance variables. Set strategic boundaries. Then spur innovation and build the right level of commitment.

As you get ready to ask the seven questions of people in your business, recall my cautions from the introduction. The questions themselves are merely raw materials. They are a means to an end. How you use them to engage the people around you will determine their value for your business.

Remember the rules of engagement:

- Ask the questions face to face. "Look me in the eye" human interaction is essential.

- Ensure that the engagement process cascades through the organization. It shouldn't be limited to the top, but instead woven into the fabric of your company.

- Involve operating managers in the process. Staff specialists can help, but their involvement should be limited to data input, facilitation, and follow-up.

- Have a healthy debate about what is right, not who is right. Ensure that everyone checks titles and office politics at the door.

- End every discussion with the most important question of all: "What are you going to do about it?"

CHECKLIST

THE SEVEN QUESTIONS (WITH FOLLOW-UP QUESTIONS)

1. Who Is Your Primary Customer?

   - Does everyone know what your primary customer values?

   - How have you organized to deliver maximum value to your customer?

   - Have you minimized resources devoted to your other constituents?

2. How Do Your Core Values Prioritize Shareholders, Employees, and Customers?

- What tough decisions have been guided by your core values?

- Do your core values recognize your business's responsibility to others?

- Is everyone committed to your core values?

3. What Critical Performance Variables Are You Tracking?

- What is your theory of value creation?

- What could cause your strategy to fail?

- How do you create accountability for performance?

4. What Strategic Boundaries Have You Set?

- What are your major reputation risks?

- Does everyone know what actions are off-limits?

- What strategic initiatives will you *not* support?

5. How Are You Generating Creative Tension?

- How are you motivating everyone to think like winning competitors?

- How do you encourage innovation across units?

- Have committees and dual reporting made your organization too complex?

6. How Committed Are Your Employees to Helping Each Other?

- What is your theory of motivation?

- How are you creating shared responsibility for success?

- How do your compensation policies affect commitment to help others?

7. What Strategic Uncertainties Keep You Awake at Night?

- How do you focus everyone's attention on these uncertainties?

- What system do you use interactively to stimulate change?

- How do you encourage bottom-up information sharing?

NOTES

Introduction

1. Thomas J. Neff and James M. Citrin, *Lessons from the Top: Search for America's Best Business Leaders* (New York: Doubleday, 1999).

Chapter 1

1. D. Grainger, "Can McDonald's Cook Again?" *Fortune*, April 12, 2003, 124.

2. Jim Cantalupo, quoted in Grainger, "Can McDonald's Cook Again?" 120.

3. Julia Werdigier, "McDonald's, but with Flair," *New York Times*, August 25, 2007.

4. Andrew Martin, "The Happiest Meal: Hot Profits," *New York Times*, January 11, 2009.

5. Janet Adamy, "McDonald's Seeks Way to Keep Sizzling," *Wall Street Journal*, March 10, 2009.

6. Hollie Shaw, "McDonald's New Recipe for Success," *Financial Post*, September 2, 2009; personal correspondence from McDonald's media relations department.

7. Martin, "The Happiest Meal."

8. Jennifer Reingold, "Home Depot's Total Rehab," *Fortune*, September 29, 2008, 159–166; Geoff Colvin, "Renovating Home Depot," *Fortune*, August 31, 2009, 45–49.

9. Michael E. Porter, *Competitive Strategy* (New York: The Free Press, 1980).

10. Bill George, *Authentic Leadership* (San Francisco: Jossey-Bass, 2004), 86.

11. Marc Gunther and Stephanie Mehta, "The Mess at AOL Time Warner," *Fortune*, May 13, 2002, 74–77.

12. Katsuaki Watanabe, "Lessons from Toyota's Long Drive," *Harvard Business Review*, July–August 2007, 74–83; Alex Taylor, "Toyota's New Man at the Wheel," *Fortune*, June 26, 2009, 82–85.

13. Josh Quittner, "How Jeff Bezos Rules the Retail Space," *Fortune*, May 5, 2008, 126–134.

14. Jeff Bezos, "The Institutional Yes," *Harvard Business Review*, October 2007, 74–82.

15. David Yoffie, "What's Your Google Strategy?" *Harvard Business Review*, April 2009, 74–81.

16. Quittner, "How Jeff Bezos Rules the Retail Space," 126–134.

17. A. G. Lafley and Ram Charan, *The Game-Changer* (New York: Crown Business, 2008), 48–49.

18. Joan S. Lublin, "Top Brass Try Life in the Trenches," *Wall Street Journal*, June 25, 2007.

19. Doreen Carvajal, "Primping for the Cameras in the Name of Research," *New York Times*, February 7, 2006.

20. L. Applegate, R. Austin, and E. Collins, "IBM's Decade of Transformation: Turnaround to Growth," Case 9-805-130 (Boston: Harvard Business School, 2009).

21. Catherine Dalton, "On Time: An Interview with FedEx's Alan B. Graf," *Business Horizons*, April 2005, 277.

22. A. G. Lafley, "What Only the CEO Can Do," *Harvard Business Review*, May 2009, 54–62; Lafley and Charan, *The Game-Changer*, 35.

23. Lafley and Charan, *The Game-Changer*.

24. Phil Patton, "Before Creating the Car, Ford Designs the Driver," *New York Times*, July 19, 2009.

25. Jeff Bezos, "The Institutional Yes."

26. Joe Nocera, "Put Buyers First? What a Concept," *New York Times*, January 5, 2008.

27. Peter T. Larsen and Jane Croft, "Visa Bows to Pressure and Unveils IPO Move," *Financial Times*, October 12, 2006.

28. Coca-Cola Co. is following a similar path. See "Coke Near Deal for Bottler," *Wall Street Journal*, February 25, 2010.

29. Michael de la Merced, "PepsiCo to Pay $7.8 Billion to Buy Its Two Top Bottlers," *New York Times*, August 5, 2009.

30. Rik Kirkland, "Cisco's Display of Strength," *Fortune*, November 12, 2007, 90–100.

31. Shawn Tully, "In This Corner! The Contender," *Fortune*, April 3, 2006, 54–66.

Chapter 2

1. Robert Simons, Kathryn Rosenberg, and Natalie Kindred, "Merck: Managing Vioxx," Cases 9-091-080 to 9-091-086 (Boston: Harvard Business School, 2009).

2. James Collins and Jerry Porras, "Building Your Company's Vision," *Harvard Business Review*, September–October 1996, 65–77.

3. Edward Wyatt, "Executives Say Fannie Mae Is Torn by Conflicting Goals," *New York Times*, April 10, 2010.

4. Simons, Rosenberg, and Kindred, "Merck: Managing Vioxx."

5. "What Makes Southwest Airlines Fly," Knowledge@Wharton, April 23, 2003.

6. Thomas J. Neff and James M. Citrin, "Herb Kelleher," *Lessons from the Top: Search for America's Best Business Leaders* (New York: Doubleday, 1999), 187–192.

7. Linda Hill, Tarun Khanna, and Emily Stecker, "HCL Technologies (A)," Case 9-408-004 (Boston: Harvard Business School, 2008).

8. Ravindra Gajulapalli and Kamalini Ramdas, "HCL Industries: Employee First, Customer Second," Case UV 1085 (Charlottesville: University of Virginia Darden Business Publishing, 2008).

9. Business Roundtable, "Principles of Corporate Governance," May 2002, 25, http://www.ecgi.org/codes/documents/brt_may2002.pdf.

10. Francesco Guerrera, "Welch Condemns Share Price Focus," *Financial Times*, March 12, 2009.

11. Neff and Citrin, *Lessons from the Top*, 334.

12. AIG Proxy Statement 2006, www.ezonlinedocuments.com/aig/2006/proxy/html2/aig_proxy2006_0017.htm.

13. Samuel J. Palmisano, "Leading Change When Business Is Good," *Harvard Business Review*, December 2004, 60–70.

14. Jessica Shambora, Adam Lashinsky, Barney Gimbel, and Julie Schlosser, "A View from the Top: The World's Most Admired Companies," *Fortune*, March 16, 2009, 105–112.

15. Jessica Dickler, "Employers: No Layoffs Here," CNNMoney .com., December 11, 2008.

16. Ray Goldberg and Hal Hogan, "Deere & Company," Case 9-905-406 (Boston: Harvard Business School, 2004).

17. Brian Hall and Rakesh Khurana, "Al Dunlap at Sunbeam," Case 9-899-218 (Boston: Harvard Business School, 2003).

18. Eugenia Levenson, "Citizen Nike," *Fortune*, November 17, 2008, 165–170.

19. Marc Gunther, "The Green Machine," *Fortune*, July 31, 2006, 42–57.

20. Exelon 2020 Strategy, www.exeloncorp.com/environment/ climatechange/overview.aspx.

21. Neff and Citrin, *Lessons from the Top*, 212–213.

Chapter 3

1. Robert Simons and Antonio Dávila, "Citibank: Performance Evaluation," Case 9-198-048 (Boston: Harvard Business School, 1999).

2. Marc Gunther, "Marriott Gets a Wake-Up Call," *Fortune*, July 6, 2009, 62–66.

3. Larry Bossidy and Ram Charan, *Execution* (New York: Crown Business, 2002), 69.

4. Thomas J. Neff and James M. Citrin, "Bossidy," *Lessons from the Top: Search for America's Best Business Leaders* (New York: Doubleday, 1999), 387.

5. John Love, *McDonald's Behind the Arches* (New York: Bantam, 1995), 110.

6. Paul B. Carroll, "Why Panic Passes Him By," *Wall Street Journal*, October 15, 2008.

7. Jeff Bezos, "The Institutional Yes," *Harvard Business Review*, October 2007, 74–82.

8. Robert Simons and Hilary Weston, "Nordstrom: Dissension in the Ranks?" Case 9-191-002 (Boston: Harvard Business School, 1990).

9. G. Miller, "The Magic Number Seven, Plus or Minus Two," *The Psychological Review* 63, no. 2 (1956): 81–97.

10. For more information on this technique, see Robert Simons, "Three Wheels of Profit Planning," *Performance Measurement & Control Systems for Implementing Strategy* (Upper Saddle River, NJ: Prentice Hall, 2000), 78–109.

11. Adam Lashinsky, "Apple: The Genius Behind Steve," *Fortune*, November 24, 2008, 70–80.

12. Mary Walsh and Jack Healy, "Ex-Chief of AIG Settles Fraud Case for $15 Million," *New York Times*, August 7, 2009.

13. Carol Loomis, "AIG: The Company That Came to Dinner," *Fortune*, January 19, 2009, 70–78.

14. Alex Taylor, "GM and Me," *Fortune*, December 8, 2008, 92–100.

15. Francesco Guerrera and Gillian Tett, "Guard of the Fortress," *Financial Times*, October 13, 2009.

16. Shawn Tully, "In This Corner! The Contender," *Fortune*, April 3, 2006, 54–66.

17. A. G. Lafley and Ram Charan, *The Game-Changer* (New York: Crown Business, 2008), 8–9.

18. Jennifer Reingold, "Home Depot's Total Rehab," *Fortune*, September 29, 2008, 159–166.

Chapter 4

1. Robert Simons and Kathryn Rosenberg, "American Cancer Society: Access to Care," Case 9-109-105 (Boston: Harvard Business School, 2008).

2. Ibid., 14.

3. Kathrine Q. Seelye, "The 'Me' in Medicare," *New York Times*, September 8, 2009.

4. William Cohan, "The Rise and Fall of Jimmy Cayne," *Fortune*, August 18, 2008, 95.

5. David Ibison, "Citigroup Apologizes to Japan," *Financial Times*, October 26, 2004.

6. Peter Lee, "What Citigroup Needs to Do Next," *Euromoney*, July 1, 2005, 1.

7. Robert Simons, "General Electric Compliance Systems" and "General Electric Valley Forge (A)–(H)," Cases 9-189-010 to 9-189-016 and 9-189-081 (Boston: Harvard Business School, 1993, 1991).

8. Paul Ingrassia, "Toyota: Too Big, Too Fast," *Wall Street Journal*, January 29, 2010.

9. Suzanne Kapner, "Changing of the Guard at Wal-Mart," *Fortune*, March 2, 2009, 68–76.

10. Joanna Pachner, "McKinsey & Co.: The Man Behind the Curtain," *Canadian Business*, February 15, 2010, 32–37.

11. Robin Dharmakumar, "Living Down a Good Name," *Forbes India*, November 11, 2009, www.forbes.com/2009/11/11/forbes-india-mckinsey.

12. http://google.com/corporate, August 11, 2009.

13. Robert Simons, Kathryn Rosenberg, and Natalie Kindred, "Sydney IVF: Stem Cell Research," Case 9-109-017 (Boston: Harvard Business School, 2009).

14. Claire Miller, "Now at Starbucks: A Rebound," *New York Times*, January 21, 2010.

15. Brad Stone, "Original Team Tries to Revive Starbucks," *New York Times*, October 30, 2008.

16. Betsy Morris, "What Makes Apple Golden," *Fortune*, March 17, 2008, 68–74.

17. David Collis and Michael Rukstad, "Can You Say What Your Strategy Is?" *Harvard Business Review*, April 2008, 82–90.

18. Alfred Sloan, *My Years with General Motors* (New York: Doubleday, 1990), 30.

19. Dennis Bakke, *Joy at Work* (Seattle, WA: PVG, 2005), 209.

20. Adam Lashinsky, "Riders on the Storm," *Fortune*, May 4, 2009, 72–80.

21. Robert Simons and Hilary Weston, "Automatic Data Processing: The EFS Decision," Case 9-190-059 (Boston: Harvard Business School, 1999). ADP's run of double-digit EPS increases spanned 1961 to 2003.

22. Geoff Colvin and Jessica Shambora, "J&J: Secrets of Success," *Fortune*, May 4, 2009, 116–121.

23. Adam Lashinsky, "Chaos by Design," *Fortune*, October 2, 2006, 86–98.

24. Vindu Goel, "Why Google Pulls the Plug," *New York Times*, February, 15, 2009.

25. Associated Press, "Johnson & Johnson Reveals Improper Payments," *International Herald Tribune*, February 13, 2007.

Chapter 5

1. Penny Singer, "New Luxury Tax Trimming Boat Sales," *New York Times*, July 21, 1991.

2. Greg Pierce, "Inside Politics: A Hard-Earned Lesson," *Washington Times*, January 7, 2003.

3. Robert Simons, "J Boats," Case 9-197-015 (Boston: Harvard Business School, 1998). All quotations in this section are from this case.

4. Andrew Grove, *Only the Paranoid Survive* (New York: Broadway, 1999), 118.

5. James C. Collins and Jerry I. Porras, "Building Your Company's Vision," *Harvard Business Review*, September–October, 1996, 65–77.

6. Alex Taylor, "GM and Me," *Fortune*, December 8, 2008, 92–100.

7. Hirotaka Takeuchi, Emi Osono, and Norihiko Shimizu, "The Contradictions That Drive Toyota's Success," *Harvard Business Review*, June 2008, 96–104.

8. Paul Carroll and Chunka Mui, *Billion-Dollar Lessons* (New York: Portfolio/Penguin, 2008).

9. Martin Fackler, "Translating the Toyota Way," *New York Times*, February 15, 2007.

10. Betsy Morris, "The New Rules," *Fortune*, July 24, 2006, 74.

11. Brian Cruver, *Anatomy of Greed* (New York: Avalon, 2002), 79.

12. Eugenia Levenson, "Citizen Nike," *Fortune*, November 24, 2008, 168.

13. Robert Simons, "ABB: The Abacus System," Case 9-192-140 (Boston: Harvard Business School, 1992).

14. Robert Simons and Kathryn Rosenberg, "American Cancer Society: Access to Care," Case 9-109-015 (Boston: Harvard Business School, 2009).

15. Robert Simons and Antonio Davila, "Siebel Systems: Organizing for the Customer," Case 9-103-014 (Boston: Harvard Business School, 2002).

16. Howard Stevenson and J. Jarillo, "A Paradigm of Entrepreneurship: Entrepreneurial Management," *Strategic Management Journal* 11, Special Issue: Corporate Entrepreneurship (Summer 1990): 23.

17. Shawn Tully, "Jamie Dimon's SWAT Team," *Fortune*, September 15, 2008, 64–78.

18. Harold Geneen, *Managing* (New York: Avon, 1984), 86.

19. Dennis W. Bakke, *Joy at Work* (Seattle, WA: PVG Publishers, 2005), 195.

20. Arlene Weintraub, "Is Merck's Medicine Working?" *BusinessWeek*, July 30, 2007, 66–70.

21. Damon Darlin, "Fiorina Had a Vision for H.P., and Some Credit for Its Turnaround," *New York Times*, October, 6, 2006.

22. Mikolaj Piskorski and Alessandro Spadini, "Procter & Gamble: Organization 2005," Case 9-707-515 (Boston: Harvard Business School, 2007).

23. Ben Worthen, "Seeking Growth, Cisco Reroutes Decisions," *Wall Street Journal*, August 6, 2009.

24. Piskorski and Spadini, "Procter & Gamble: Organization 2005."

25. If you're interested in how to design a matrix properly, see Chapter 8 in Robert Simons, *Levers of Organization Design* (Boston: Harvard Business School Press, 2005).

Chapter 6

1. Kevin and Jackie Freiberg, *Nuts: Southwest Airlines' Crazy Recipe for Business and Personal Success* (New York: Broadway Books, 1998), 290; James Parker, "The Ten-Minute Turnaround," in *Do the Right Thing* (Upper Saddle River, NJ: Wharton School Publishing, 2008), 39–46.

2. Greg Hasell, "The Fall of Enron: The Culture," *Houston Chronicle*, December 9, 2001.

3. Loren Fox, *Enron: The Rise and Fall* (Hoboken, NJ: Wiley, 2003), chapter 5.

4. Hassell, "The Fall of Enron"; Fox, *Enron*, 86.

5. Ken Iverson, *Plain Talk* (New York: Wiley, 1998), 83.

6. Steven Kerr, "On the Folly of Hoping for A While Rewarding B," *Academy of Management Journal* 18, no. 4 (1975): 769–783.

7. Douglas McGregor, *The Human Side of Enterprise* (New York: McGraw-Hill, 1960).

8. Fox, *Enron*, 79.

9. Robert Simons and Hilary Weston, "Mary Kay Cosmetics: Sales Force Incentives," Case 9-190-103 (Boston: Harvard Business School, 1999).

10. Thomas A. Stewart and Bronwyn Fryer, "Cisco Sees the Future," *Harvard Business Review,* November 2008, 72–79.

11. Nanette Byrnes, "The Art of Motivation," *BusinessWeek*, May 1, 2006, 56.

12. Robert Simons and Kathryn Rosenberg, "American Cancer Society: Access to Care," Case 9-109-015 (Boston: Harvard Business School, 2009).

13. James Parker, *Do the Right Thing* (Upper Saddle River, NJ: Wharton School Publishing, 2008), 109.

14. Iverson, *Plain Talk*, 102.

15. Ibid., 55.

16. Jeff Bailey, "Southwest. Way Southwest," *New York Times*, February 13, 2008.

17. Parker, *Do the Right Thing*, 52.

18. Iverson, *Plain Talk*, 107.

19. Parker, *Do the Right Thing*, 111, 160.

20. Carol Loomis, "AIG: The Company That Came to Dinner," *Fortune*, January 19, 2009, 70–78.

21. Roger Lowenstein, "Alone at the Top," *New York Times Magazine*, August 27, 2000, 32.

22. Timothy Schellhardt, "A Marriage of Unequals," *Wall Street Journal*, April 8, 1999.

23. J. S. Lublin, "Executive Pay (A Special Report). Net Envy," *Wall Street Journal*, April 6, 2000.

24. Sarah Anderson, John Cavanagh, Chuck Collins, and Sam Pizzigati, "Executive Excess 2008: How Average Taxpayers Subsidize Runaway Pay. 15th Annual CEO Compensation Survey," (Washington, DC: Institute for Policy Studies, 2008). Also, Jerry Useem, "The Winner-Steal-All Society," *The American Prospect Magazine*, October 21, 2002, 13–14.

25. "What Makes Southwest Airlines Fly," Knowledge@Wharton, April 23, 2003.

26. Joe Brancatelli, "Southwest Airlines's Seven Secrets for Success," Portfolio.com, July 8, 2008.

27. Iverson, *Plain Talk*, 15.

28. Jeffrey O'Brien, "IBM's Grand Plan to Save the Planet," *Fortune*, May 4, 2009, 84–91.

Chapter 7

1. Geoff Colvin and Jessica Shambora, "J&J: Secrets of Success," *Fortune*, May 4, 2009, 116–121.

2. Thomas J. Neff and James M. Citrin, *Lessons from the Top: Search for America's Best Business Leaders* (New York: Doubleday, 1999), 210.

3. Robert Simons and Antonio Davila, "ATH MicroTechnologies: Making the Numbers," Case 9-108-091 (Boston: Harvard Business School, 2009).

4. Stephanie Mehta, "Can AOL Keep Pace?" *Fortune*, August 21, 2006, 29–30.

5. Larry Bossidy and Ram Charan, *Confronting Reality* (New York: Crown Business, 2004), 218.

6. Harold Geneen, *Managing* (New York: Avon, 1984), 106.

7. Ibid.

8. Joe Nocera, "Risk Management," *New York Times Magazine*, January 4, 2009.

9. Jenny Anderson, "As Goldman Thrives, Some Say Ethos Fades," *New York Times*, December 16, 2009; "Goldman Employees Rally Around Blankfein," *New York Times*, April 20, 2010.

10. Bossidy and Charan, *Confronting Reality*, 189.

11. Robert Simons, "Strategic Orientation and Top Management Attention to Control Systems," *Strategic Management Journal* 12, no. 1 (January 1991): 49–62.

12. Scott Malone, "How Talking the Talk Can Transform a Firm," *Boston Globe*, January 27, 2008.

13. Robert Simons and Hilary Weston, "Automatic Data Processing," Case 9-190-059 (Boston: Harvard Business School, 1989).

14. Louise Story and Landon Thomas, "Tales from Lehman's Crypt," *New York Times*, September 13, 2009.

15. Andrew S. Grove, *Only the Paranoid Survive* (New York: Currency/Doubleday, 1996), 119.

16. Shawn Tully, "Jamie Dimon's Swat Team," *Fortune*, September 15, 2008.

17. Alex Taylor, "Fixing Up Ford," *Fortune,* May 25, 2009, 49.

18. Neff and Citrin, *Lessons from the Top*, 214.

19. Robert Simons, "Codman & Shurtleff: Planning and Control System," Case 9-187-081 (Boston: Harvard Business School, 2000).

INDEX

ACKNOWLEDGMENTS

This book was twenty-five years in the making. I cannot do justice here to all the people who helped guide my thinking over these many years. But I can single out— and thank—those people without whom this book would never have been written.

The project began when acquisition editor Kirsten Sandberg pitched the idea of a book based on questions to her Harvard Business Press colleagues, and ended with production editor Allison Peter shepherding the manuscript through final copyediting and page proofs. In between, Ania Wieckowski applied her considerable editorial skills to reviewing numerous drafts, proposing changes and clarifications, and helping make the ideas accessible to you, the reader.

Research associates Kathryn Rosenberg and Natalie Kindred played important roles in gathering material to support the arguments in the book, as well as offering suggestions for improving the presentation. Heidi May, my assistant, helped manage my schedule to keep the project on track.

Many people provided valuable feedback on drafts, including my Harvard colleagues Ray Gilmartin, David Hawkins, Michele Jurgens, Jay Lorsch, Warren McFarlan, Asís Martinez-Jerez, and (especially) Tom Piper. David Champion at *Harvard Business Review* contributed important insight about the best way to present the questions. My mentor and teacher, Henry Mintzberg, also gave me constructive feedback, as did my two sons, James and Ian. Judy, my wife, listened patiently as I worked out the ideas, questioned and tested my thinking, and, as always, encouraged me along the way.

Dean Jay Light provided greatly appreciated resources and support during difficult times.

But this book could never have been written—because I would not be here to write it—without the extraordinary skill and care of the doctors and staff at Dana Farber Cancer Institute and Brigham and Women's Hospital, especially Dr. Tom Clancy, Dr. Harvey Mamon, Dr. Jeff Myerhardt, and Dr. Mike Zinner.

My heartfelt thank you to all.

ABOUT THE AUTHOR

ROBERT SIMONS is the Charles M. Williams Professor of Business Administration at Harvard Business School. Over the last twenty-five years, Simons has taught accounting, management control, and strategy implementation courses in both the Harvard MBA and Executive Education Programs. He has served as chairman of Harvard's Advanced Management Program and cochair of the Driving Corporate Performance program, and has developed two MBA courses: Achieving Profit Goals and Strategies, and Designing Organizations for Performance.

Simons is the author of three earlier books: *Levers of Control, Levers of Organization Design*, and *Performance Measurement and Control Systems for Implementing Strategy*. His ongoing research into the relationship between business strategy, organization design, and management control systems has been published in management journals such as *Harvard Business Review*, *Sloan Management Review*, and *Strategic Management Journal*.

A Canadian chartered accountant, Simons earned his PhD from McGill University. He has testified as an expert witness in U.S. Federal Court and served as a consultant to companies around the world.